AfterBurn

AfterBurn
essays built from heat and ashes

by Rebecca Evans

~ 2025 ~

AfterBurn
© Copyright 2026 Rebecca Evans
All rights reserved. No part of this book may be used or reproduced in any manner whatsoever without written permission from either the author or the publisher, except in the case of credited epigraphs or brief quotations embedded in articles or reviews.

Editor-in-chief
Eric Morago

Operations Associate
Shelly Holder

Associate Editors
Mackensi E. Green
Allysa Murray
Ellen Webre

Copy Editor
Betty Rodgers

Editor Emeritus
Michael Miller

Cover design
Eric Morago

Book design
Michael Wada

Moon Tide logo design
Abraham Gomez

AfterBurn
is published by Moon Tide Press

Moon Tide Press
6709 Washington Ave. #9297
Whittier, CA 90608
www.moontidepress.com

FIRST EDITION

Printed in the United States of America

ISBN # 978-1-957799-40-7

Further Praise for *AfterBurn*

Rebecca Evans is neither a victor or a soul steeped in lament, but a survivor whose testimony is a compelling and contemplative dissertation on how to be a human in a world that tries to crush you. War, abuse, trauma, crisis of health both of the body and the mind, *AfterBurn* offers the deep wisdom of someone who dares to exist in power and poetry and raise her voice to say I'm still here. These essays offer inspiration through the potency of truth and vulnerability and will stick with a reader long after the last page is turned.

— Alan Heathcock, author, *Volt*

"Writing will change me, alter my course, reshaping the arc of my own narrative" writes Rebecca Evans, and this searing, startling, deeply inspiring collection will do the same for readers—it will change and alter and help readers reshape their own narratives. This is a book of profound reckoning and healing, a book about facing hard truths and delicately cradling the beauty and peace we can find after we walk through our own fire. We're so lucky to have Rebecca Evans' voice in the world—her courage and wisdom shine through every page.

— Gayle Brandeis, author, *Drawing Breath: Essays on Writing, the Body, and Loss*

Rebecca Evans' essays are as raw, honest and emotionally evocative as any I have read. She has a unique talent for combining beautiful, poetic prose with transparent and deeply relatable revelations about what makes us human.

— Brendan Spiegel, Co-Founder & Director, *Narratively Literary Magazine*

Rebecca Evans's *AfterBurn* invites readers into a deeply personal landscape, one shaped by the quiet battles of memory and resilience. Through these flash essays, which border on prose poetry, Evans explores the complexities of trauma, motherhood, and the persistent search for a sense of self. It's a stirring collection that offers thoughtful reflections on the enduring human spirit.

— Peter Mountford, author, *Detonator,*
A Young man's Guide to Late Capitalism

If attention is a commodity, what happens when a relentlessly curious mind pays attention to the everyday life of a single mother, a survivor of domestic violence, and a woman warrior? This: the reader reaps the dividends of a powerful testament to a lifelong fight full of equal parts tenderness and rage. *AfterBurn* is a lyrical and formally inventive memoir, a love letter to the author's sons and to herself, a scream into the void where the echoes keep bouncing back, demanding an ear. And if you're listening, you can hear Evans take her traumas and triumphs and turn them into something alchemical and undeniably inspirational. You can hear her restless heart pound and her mind spin around. If you're listening, you get paid back from this book in ways you can't even imagine.

— Steven Church, author, *I'm Just Getting to the Disturbing Part*

Wisdom, strength, pain, resilience, and joy flow from these essays by Rebecca Evans. Her craft, unflinching honesty, and inspiring voice in *AfterBurn* become conversations, allowing us to reflect upon our own suffering, love, discoveries, and healing on this shared path called life. Immerse yourself in these lyrical gems of humanity and marvel at the light they cast.

— Guy Biederman, author, *Translated From The Original,*
one-inch punch fiction

In her collection of essays and poems, *AfterBurn*, Rebecca Evans empties it all. A life's panorama of agony and ecstasy rendered to imagery and action. She dumps it all: Brain box, Kurdistan, Berlin Wall, London, cornfields in Indiana, cold concrete floors in Boise. War, dignity, birth, family, trauma, decency, horror, redemption, joy. *AfterBurn* is a work of art.

— Ken Rodgers, film producer, *Bravo! Uncommon Men, Uncommon Valor*

Unwavering in its commitment to emotional honesty, Rebecca's essays dare to explore the darker corners of the human experience with compassion and tenderness. As she does so, she inevitably finds ways to return us to the light by celebrating life's small victories. In prose that's equal parts hypnotic and limpid, she deftly surveys the past and the present only to invite her reader to be inspired by her bravery and do the same.

— Cory Schneider, Brooklyn fiction writer and essayist

Contents

Foreword by Harrison Salow	14
It doesn't matter	16
Still Things	17
We Hold Our Breath as We Pass the Lunchroom	20
A Decent Day	22
Buddy Check	25
Storage	27
How We Wait	30
Push	33
Blurred	36
When Fireflies Scatter	40
War Zoning with a Toddler on My Back	42
I'm the Deadliest	46
We Leave Our Signature in Cement	50
RePrints for a Poet	52
Writing "Me"	55
A Little Letter from an AI Rebutter	58
When a Bear Isn't Mentioned in Your Horoscope	61
WaPo Horoscope—Cancer, Sept 28th, 2024	64
Boosters	66
Hand-Off	69
Piggybacking the Smallest Wrestler	72
Re-Womb	75
What if Your C-Section Inspired Your Child's Need to Escape	77
Sticks for Gears	80
Earthworms Fatter Than the Year Before	82
Thanks for Sharing the Armrest	85
Cooking Instructions	88
Forging	91
Afterwards	94
Somewhere in Star, Idaho, Between Rage and Comfort	97
…Sauntering…	99
Feather Sweeping in Gary, Indiana, 1986	102
Play Me Some Willie	104

Unlinear Me	107
Finding Myself in the Middle of a Row	110
AfterBurn	112
Tarnished	114
Chiseled	117
Cardamon & Caraway	119
The Power of a Pseudonym	122
The Price of Energy	124
Decluttering Damages My Writing	128
Berry-Picking Meditation	131
Epilogue	*132*
About the Author	*133*
Acknowledgments	*134*

To My Younger Self

Foreword

This compellingly time-woven prose-poem—a series of syncopated vignettes showcasing a fascinating life—
might well be called a tapestry, were it written by someone else. But Rebecca Evans' *AfterBurn* would not be well served by such a description.

These strands of life are woven not with silk and wool, but with blood, bone, sinew and sweat; by suffering and affliction; by resolution and perseverance - held together by vision, fortitude and immense courage. The afterimage that arises from this painfully triumphant verse is less a cohesive panorama than a fortress, ringed with thorns and brambles, that houses the heartbeat of a mother, a soldier, an artist, a survivor, a Jew.

"I understand the way I belong in the world. The way I fold into these crevices with men and boys. Understand that most women do not like me. Understand that I am an outlier – not quite veteran enough, disabled enough, Jewish enough…I accept the way women leave me uneasy—no matter their kindness—I've trouble aligning…"

And yet it was men who battered. Men who assaulted. Men who raped. Men who betrayed. In Rebecca's singular and burning story, how this painful history is reconciled with the bearing, birthing, raising of men, is a revelation of epic resurrection. It is searing. It is also tender. It is harrowing. It is also transfixing.

Each page builds upon the next, chronicling Rebecca's journey through a half-century of disability, poverty, achievement, elevation, wisdom, and ultimate success. A poignant tribute to survival, personal power, heroism, and fierce, relentless love.

The second time you read it, you will see miracles.

The first time, you just won't believe it.

— Harrison Solow, PhD

Dr Solow is an award-winning author, Pushcart Prize Essayist, Literature and Writing Professor, University Press Editor, Writer for the Professions, Theologian, Poet, Fixer, Mother, and Friend.

It doesn't matter

if I've a new lump on the right—wait, let me look—left. It's on the left side of my nose. One more facial imperfection equals another badge of honor distinguishing my body map, engraving my journey.

if I get it all done and, in my trying, I come undone.

if others never say, *Sorry*—like (insert list of names here)—so long as I do.

if you see me as weak or superhuman. What matters is the way I see myself and whether I risk doing what's needed to keep water running, lights on, my family clothed, fed.

if I feel safe so long as anyone in my presence knows they are safe with me.

if I sleep in shards and bursts or through an entire afternoon.

if my body believes she's rested, she is. And if my body is tired, she is.

if my body wants to keep going when my heart and head are weary or worn and I pause. And in my pause, I might wonder, *Have I ever existed without experiencing a worn mind or weary heart*? And, *Did I use up all my beats on worry or rage*?

if your political lens leans differently than mine, so long as we can sit at a table and speak our minds with openness and respect and still find, no, still hunt for center ground and always, always agree to do what's best for the children.

if you know me. Know that we've met at some point, someplace, sometime. I'm that hungry dog or protective mamma or unbreathing boy or wrongly touched toddler. I'm the diva on the dance floor with a glow stick for a necklace who quits caring for one hour as the pain finally flees her body. She melts into all the other earth-drum-dancers pounding pain from their veins, blending into one because remembering is all that matters in the end—all that remains, all that joins us, often burns.

Still Things

If I stand still long enough, she will come, tangle in my lashes, leave a trail of kisses, and wisp my wishes into truth. What is desire if not truth transmitted from sun to the ancients and back again?

We're lucky it—truth—finds us.

Moving things push through still things.

At the river yesterday, my leashed pup pulled me in her enchantment. We moved through land as if we owned it, as if we owned it all. She—Penelope—pranced and paused and I kept seeking sky through the umbrella of branches, every step offering new perspective. The river rippled, running alongside us and I was unsure who kept up with whom. Though, not anymore. Not today. I can't say if there's such a thing as *Keeping Up*. Or *Catching Up*. Or finishing—truly finishing—anything.

Still things gather the movers.

In the middle of the night, her whiskers flicker my cheeks. She pats my head as if I need petting. I probably do. She presses her nose to my nose. I wake but do not move. I do not dare. If I blink, I know she'll quit and, *Oh!* How I cherish this calico mid-night love. (It's more than love.) It's absorption—one being into another, into another—like Russian nesting dolls. Like the way we soak into each other, skin to sweat to spit, and hurt to hangryness to healing.

Moving things rarely notice still things.

Tonight offers Earth's longest day. Here, Idaho, sun hangs in sky—magenta and mango—reaching an untouchable part of me. I stretch and sunbathe at nine pm, long after I'm filled: chai and pasta and a crunchy salad mixed with pecans and cranberries. We're told, *Avoid sunbathing.* I ask you, whose advice are you willing to absorb?

Still things notice most things.

This morning, I try to curate a list of still things. I cannot. I could not. Nothing seems still. And now, nothing seems to die. Instead, every thing dwells in this continuous state of rebirth. Think about it. Cottonwood fluff lands on your eyelashes and you blink it away. Dust remains. Your body drinks it in. Over time, you become a bit of cottonwood.

Moving things notice less.

The ants dot into a line, marching towards home or food or following your ladybug, the one you waited for when you thought you were still—though you were not. Your blood pulsed and your temperature maintained while you swallowed, swigging in a bit of earth and even more airborne ash. The milkweed currently grows. The strawberry deepens her crimson hue. Your son softly snores one room over, reminding you that you no longer need to check his chest, watch for the rise and fall, like the way you hovered when he held more fragility. Someone turns an engine. Someone else lights a flame for a simple soup. All the while coffee slow-drips to life in a mug shaped from clay and soot and calloused hands. Someone's baby gulps his final breath. Still the NICU machines keep beeping, and the nurses rush as sound seeps into the empty—though not empty—hospital halls. Somewhere else, someone gives birth on the floor in a bathroom stall, and she clenches more shame than pain. A hurricane. A multi-vortexed tornado walks earth. Lightning showers. An athlete dips into an ice bath, believing she's in control. You lick your lips, but you don't think of this as movement. All the while, the fridge hums and so does your head, worried about medical debt. There's a small girl with a bomb strapped to her chest, her hand-me-down dress was once her sister's. Maybe she is five. If she lived across the street, she'd attend school, and she would still not be safe. Across the world, a war. Another in your backyard. And one more at your neighborhood Shop and Carry. There's one in your heart—war, that is—but you won't look at that. You want to believe, believe that you can sprawl across the bounty of a red-capped mushroom, sink into her white spots, become something else if you're still enough. Or perhaps you believe your stillness will help you unnotice the moving things, the continuous pulse around and within you.

Here, in your sunbathing solstice ritual, you let your ladybug lace through your lashes, let her leave traces so you can later devour aphids and rescue a single rose.

We Hold Our Breath as We Pass the Lunchroom

My red string bikini, which I don't know as a string, clings, thanks to baby oil. We tan on the dunes, Lake Michigan, splay our arms into wings and wishes, like snow angels but with sand. We hope for contrast—dark against light—as we check our bottoms' hems. We hope to turn ourselves into something sexy. Hope to turn our bodies into new nations. We are 14 and still filled with hope.

The hot-white sun bleaches my hair so light it seems transparent. Along with my string, I don a six-pack and biceps as I've push-upped my way through that tiny portal between middle and high school, though I long for a round ass, like Rachel McGlish. In the mornings, I run three miles on the cinder-road route outside our subdivision. I obey my coach. No. Not my coach. Coach T, the boys' track coach who offers to help me after practice.

I'll teach you to explode, he says, and, *Make you a champion.*

I follow his canon, believe his promises that if I do what he says, I'll get ahead in life and track. When he touches my thighs, shows up at my home at ten pm, kisses me in the rain, I still want to win.

When not at the dunes, we detassel corn or pick asparagus or peel papery outer layers of onions so large and yellow you'd think them melons. Dressed in halters or tube tops and shorts, we walk the fields. We smolder our flesh, scorch our scalps. Corn stalk blades cut crisp across our bare bellies. By summer's end, we hope for acknowledgement, *You've the best tan, girl.* We are midwestern culture in the early '80s, the place where pig farms rule and boys steer tractors before they legally access driving permits.

When not at the dunes, I roll my bikini into a ball. It fits in my palm. I stash it in my sock drawer. The same way I hide my lunch money, skipping food in order to buy track spikes and cheerleading Keds. The suit stays secreted through winter. And during winter, I teach my body to deny herself her desires. We—my body and me—hold our breath as we pass the lunchroom, especially on tater tot or pizza days.

• The next summer, when not at the dunes, we douse more oil and spread blankets or beach towels on our tacky tar roofs. We sprawl our bodies, turn our feet outward, hoping our inner thighs gather sun. We don't yet know to think about frying our skin. We fail to consider the damage of blisters. We carry no foresight of wrinkles or cancer. Most of us don't believe we'll make it—make it out of Indiana. Make it to middle age.

A Decent Day

4 am yesterday: I'm fine. Dialed in. I rinse my hands, my face, lotion up. I wear hand-me-down cow slippers gifted to me from my adult son.

5 am: After I journal, I snap fresh linens onto my king. I urge my four Newfies off my bed four times. There may or may not be bluebirds on my shoulder.

6 am: I feed my Newfies, sweep their trails of food from laundry room to back door, refill their water seven times. I remember to feed our cat, Cali, because she howls down the hall. I hope she doesn't feel abandoned. Again.

6:17 am: I perform my own yoga-flow-rise-and-roll. I offer myself to me and sing with Sinéad O'Connor's "Thank You for Hearing Me" on repeat.

7 am: I gulp a handful of vitamins, open blinds, turn off outside lights, flame tea candles in oil burners scented with linen, lemon, basil.

7:12 am: I arrange breakfast for my sons and, since it's a weekend, I include settings for their friends. A basket of bagels, rows of jams and honeys and flavored cream cheeses. I leave a Post It, *Eat Up!*

7:18 am: I launch my laundry—six loads, three weeks' worth. I used to "keep up" with these small tasks. Now I allow piles to bloom, accepting there's no such beast as "catching up."

7:30 am: I crawl into my fresh-sheeted bed, wake at 10:15 am.

NOTE TO SELF: I remember to Zoom, a workshop with Carmen Maria Machada. I dress in something other than pajamas. In workshop, a colleague reads her first draft aloud. I listen, mouth gaping. I'm thankful I kept my hand down, because, *holy shit*, the rush of inadequacy layers thick like a slab of butter.

I remember, *I forgot to eat.* After class, I prep avocado toast—a slice of rosemary bread with smashed avocado. I drizzle basil oil and a pinch of flakey salt on top.

Noon: I pull a smorgasbord of leftovers for the hungry man-cub crew—spaghetti and hamburgers and home fries. I add cans of flavored water in a bin with ice and set out reuseable straws.

1 pm: I handwash dishes. One of my meditations. Now, my hands throb. My forearms scream. My skin jolts, bites. Not from dishwashing but from nerve pain.

1:23 pm: I stretch. I stretch in silence. I stretch my neck and piriformis. I return to bed. Sleep on top of my covers. Hope for a quick nap. *Don't waste time.*

3:17 pm: I'm up. I move laundry from washer to dryer to bed. I fold. I keep laundry moving. I can keep only my laundry moving.
Between small tasks and smaller moments, I long for my bed. My body moves like clouds on a still day. Every task, once mindless, once sideshows of my hyper-productive life. Here, they feel like Olympic feats: watering indoor plants, gathering mail, folding creases in blue jeans.

What I want is to write. Write and write and write in-between my almost-living. No. I want to write first drafts like my colleague.

The kind of prose that leaves my own mouth agape.
I'm down, back in bed at **4:15**. Awake at **5:15**. And **6**. And **6:20**.

Dinner: I curate a spread much like a pizza factory, including chef hats and aprons. The man-cubs, giddy, end up coated in sauce and parmesan. The Newfies lick my sons' shoes.

7 pm: I feed my Newfies. I feed my cat. I keep moving laundry.

7:30 pm: After dinner and dishes and another load of socks, I challenge myself, *Organize one thing. Ten poems into ten pages. You have ten poems. Do this. Rest later.*

8 pm: I try.

8:53 pm: I fail.

9 pm: I submit. Not my poems.

9:45 pm: I light a candle, smudge sage and Santo Paolo, ring my singing bowl, and sit, but only for a short time. Under five, give or take.

10 pm: I bathe, submerge into salted chamomile waters, pat dry, pull on flannel and my heated lavender booties.

10:20 pm: In bed.

11:30 pm: I bolt with a story. A Russian soldier or marine and the nearness of war. My sons and their friends play Monopoly or Clue or Risk at our kitchen table, safe and bubbled from the doom outside, and I note:
 I did it.
 I cared for my sons, my pets, my home. I tended to myself, my writing as best I could. A significant life equates our best attempts within our limits. Means allowing bits of dignity and decency. Means offering latitude to not "measure up." Means ceasing our worry over *being enough* and *doing enough* and, instead, delicately cradling this one decent day. Hold it in your palm, like a fallen finch who crashed into your window and you thought her dead, but now, *See?* Here, a flicker from her wing.

Midnight: I feel good. Not great. Not my body. Just my heart. Better. Not bad.

Buddy Check

I'm better than I used to be, I say, replying to my grown son's question about my lock-checking ways.
But how many times a night? he asks.
Every few hours. You know...better.
Better than what? he asks.
I sit taller.
Who cares if I check and uncheck doors and windows? Who does this hurt? It brings me peace. It's not damaging. It's not illegal. Does it matter? You know I walked through a war, right? You know I endured 40 surgeries with your disabled brother? You know I fled your father and, after, his hit man who tailed me for almost two years? So I'm a tad vigilant. I've earned it. Like my right to pee frequently since birthing three boys.

*

I pick my face. Not really my face. My skin. No. That's not accurate either. I squeeze my pores. I've this need to squeeze sebaceous filament—a bleed of oil and dead skin. Once, when strep traveled from my throat to my ear to my mastoid—that honeycomb bone near your nape—the surgeon carved a small incision, placed a tube, laid me on my side for weeks, allowing infection to drip through my ear and out of my head. They couldn't cut me open. Couldn't slice that bone. Everything too near the brain. My ear dripped, saturating my pillow for months. I told myself, *My brain seeps the lies I've absorbed: I'm too big, too old, too dumb, too much, too little, too poor, too driven, too loud.* I read and re-read two books, *I Will Not Die an Unlived Life* and *The Invitation*, while my toddler-sons pillow-fought at the foot of my bed.

While lying on my right side, draining and draining and draining, I knew I needed to flee that marriage. Knew I needed to write my stories. Knew my stories could not fit through my tiny fistula. Believed my pen might save me. This was 2006. It took four more years of gathering for me to leave. I gathered documents, like my sons' birth certificates, in safe deposit boxes. Gathered counseling sessions, an exodus plan, and my grandmother's recipe box.

When my husband said, *I'll bury you if you leave,* adding, *Because I love you,* I believed him.

I believed in his ability to bring me more damage. This, my final gathering.

*

When anxious, I cocoon myself. I hear, *Take cover* and, *Do a buddy check.* These words, once sounded with alarms during wartime training. A buddy check includes masking up, diving beneath something heavy, feeling around for injured comrades, and, if you find one, dragging them to safety. Today, I am my own buddy. I cover. I take cover. I'm under cover. I build a blanket fort on my king-size bed, though I still sleep only on the edge. I tell myself, *The rest of my bed is for books and snacks and pups.* While beneath my covers, I read or play Sudoku. This, my mind distraction. This, before I spiral into inked oceans of rumination. I tell myself, *This thinking helps me stay prepared.* I know better. I know that thinking keeps me crawling through glass, keeps me small.

While under covers, I fetal myself, grow smaller and smaller and smaller. As a child, I curled this way, saying to my little self, *If I grow small enough the spider on the ceiling won't bite.* I didn't know the spider was Daddy. Was Mother. Would become my husband. Was and is still webbing corners in my mind.

Under cover, I wait for my chin to rise. Wait for my eyes to tip down. Wait for my self-hating to come. I check, I squeeze, I cover. These little tics are involuntary responses, like my heartbeats or eye blinks, my reaction to the storm, the wind, the world. And this, this is ok. This is my ok.

Storage

In the military, I called it my brain box.

They—the military—trained us to store emotions. Trained us to focus.

Handle your shit, they'd say. So we did. I did. Management meant storage. I learned to shove my shit in that box while I shoveled forkfuls of food, binging and purging. I learned to numb.

I exited the military in 1993 and my first brain box cracked in 2010.

Try to remember your first heartbreak or death or hefty loss—months of crying, your face puffed, that continuous sting of bile.

Here, 2010, I tape up garbage bags in my garage. I tape because I'm not safe. My sons are not safe. This is Idaho and no protection order will protect us. My ex is on a mission to bury me. His hitman follows me. Okay, that's an exaggeration. The hitman is really a friend of my ex who went to prison for solicitation for murder. It's easier to call him *Hitman*. I feel a red dot marking my forehead or heart. I feel like prey. All. The. Time. I catch myself praying, chanting Mother Marys. I forget I'm Jewish.

I stretch an army-green lawn bag over my garage windows, duct-taping the bag at each corner. The witness protection team from Meridian Police suggested this. As I tape, something flashes. It might be army-green war, duffels, body bags. Then I see him. The boy. I'm back in Iraq. I'm pumping his chest. His chest is still. I am not.

Still. I pump.

I say, *Comeoncomeoncomeon.*

I see me failing. Failing that boy. The boy. The boy. I kneel on the garage floor, duct tape in hand.

I see the bloody handprint on the shattered windscreen of the F-111.

I remember asking, *Is that Jerry's?* wondering if the print belongs to my pilot friend.

I remember someone saying, *He crashed to save the small village.*

I see the wall. No. I don't. I don't see the wall. I feel the wall. No. That's not right. I feel my face on the concrete floor in the garage.

I feel the wall and remember my face hitting the wall.

Remember my face mashing into the wall and my wondering, *Why can't I move?* I remember hearing my panties rip and how dark the hallway turned as the Navy dude thrust himself into me. I remember not knowing he was Navy until after, when I smoothed my skirt and looked at his cap.

I remember thinking, *Who'll believe me?*

Thinking, *And this? In the middle of a fucking war?*

I fetal on my garage floor. I hear a howl and wonder, *Coyote?* And the howl keeps going. The hairs on my body rise and I am no longer numb. I'm a wounded animal. I'm giving birth. I've found some exit wound and the opening widens. There's no place to apply pressure. I'm bleeding out.

I couldn't tell you how long I remained cocooned, gripping that roll of duct tape. An hour? Five? I sobbed until I dry-heaved. I heaved until I emptied. At some point, I understood the howling was me and I chewed through the collar of my tee. My voice turned to a whisper.

My sons, away at school. My disengaged family, outside of Idaho. There, on that floor, curled alone. There was no one to hold me, pat my back, say, *There, there.*

Except there was.

Me.

Today, 2025, my garage has a second fridge, a home gym, and two filing cabinets. The drawers, neatly divided, labeled, and alphabetized: Food Stamps, IRS, Scholarships. A folder for each son's school records. Medical documents, organized by year and procedure. My now-adult disabled son has endured 40 surgeries. I'm circling near 15 of my own, give or take.

I tell you this because I want you to see my brain, neatly categorized and quite stunningly systematic.

My ex once bragged during our high-conflict mediation, *She can deliver any document in under three minutes.*

It's the only nice thing I remember him saying about me.

When I tell you, *This is my brain*, I'm not exactly honest. These are sections of my brain box. These are slow and careful undoings of trauma and military training. These are the parts I believe I can manage or, perhaps control. This seems the way for me, the way to empty out of my body what I can, when I can.

You don't need to know this, but I need to tell you that my youngest, now 16, still visits my ex, his father, but with supervision. He visits only once a month. After, as we drive home following each visit, we pause for ice cream or a smoothie—our unspoken transition out of conflict and into home. Once home, we gather as family, we cook, usually pasta. We watch another mindless episode on Netflix. Our Newfoundlands drape over our bodies. A lavender candle blazes one room over. Our address remains unlisted. Our blinds, sealed. Our garage holds my stories but has no windows. I have no need to tape up lawn bags.

How We Wait

Between November 2009 and March 2010, I wait to leave my now-ex-husband. While waiting, I push earbuds deep and run my curated playlist of 12 songs on repeat. This music feels like my life soundtrack and churns into my mantra. I can't tell you how Josh Groban's "Vincent" ended up alongside "Can Anybody Hear Her?" and "Revelation," but to this day, when I hear any of those tunes, I rock. When I say, *Rock,* I mean, arms wrapped around myself, cradle-like, a return to the time I waited and swayed, tending my youngest boy, not yet a year old.

    back

In that waiting, I place important documents—business invoices, phone records, tax forms—between sneakers and sports bras in my gym bag. I sneak my backpack to a friend who copies and then returns the originals. I carefully re-place each document. Like a spy. Like a criminal. Like a bad warrior.

    and

One afternoon, between aforementioned November and March, I meet a different friend at Les Schwab in Nampa, Idaho. No, I did not need my tires aired, changed, aligned. Instead, I hand her my military duffle packed with medical supplies for my three sons: a nebulizer, a pacemaker recording device, Xopenex, Albuterol, and diapers.

    forth

Later that night, my then-husband asks, *What did you do to the tires on our Denali?* Who knew he placed a tracker on my car? A tracer on my phone? We—my friend and me—had noted a man in a black truck parked across the way, also waiting. The man—(insert name here)—had once been imprisoned for solicitation for murder. Today, I simply say, *A hitman followed me.* It never felt an exaggeration, but today it feels like someone else's story.

back

Waiting to leave a bad marriage is like snipping your way through a spider web one strand at a time. You never know when the right time to flee will be. You listen to your pulse, your playlist, your ruminating mind. The challenge is your deafness. You cannot hear. Anything. You cannot hear because you hold your breath, and this holding proves too loud.

In my waiting, I knew none of this.

and

This type of waiting is much like war. Ask any soldier and they will tell you, *Much of my time in war was spent waiting.* Ask any wife imprisoned and she'll nod, *Waiting was the main event in my hostile marriage.* You wait for the words, the punch, the threat, the punishment. When they don't come at the expected time, the waiting worsens. It's worse because you understand your enemy has advanced and is now four moves ahead. You have lost his rhythm, his predictability.

forth

A good enemy is like a bad husband. They hold the line with unpredictability. Their ability to maintain chaos is an art, a song, a last lingering note. What you know is that you can no longer carry your continuous bracing for blows. It's less than good when you say to yourself, *I can take a punch.* Especially when you recite this every morning. You've forgotten your original mantra, the one you were born with.

back

What you know is that once you release your guard, you become your most vulnerable—in the shower, in your sleep, rocking your babe. Here, the enemy strikes. Later, long after the leaving, even longer after the waiting, your infant is now a teen and still you wake at three am and comfort yourself through the rocking back and forth.

Peace feels fleeting. You remain braced. Some day, some where, in the center of a poem, you find a line that explains your erratic pulse. You errand—to the post office, the bank, the library—noting the way you shift your weight. Foot to foot,

back and forth.

You accept this, this act of solace, your meditation. Your request through rhythms and body hums. No matter if anybody hears your soundtrack. No matter if anyone reads the lines above your brow. No matter if you rock, natural as the ebb and flow of tide and turmoil. The final thread of the web slips away and you,
you unhold your breath.

Push

I thought, *How strong this boy. See the wall of muscle he moves?*

He expanded my fascia and ligaments simply to grow. When I say, *Expand*, what I mean is near-rupture. Only a few months prior, I'd landed an aerial turn toe-touch into a split, my left leg forward, my right extended behind. When you land this element, you lean forward, press ribs to thigh and "catch" your body with your hands, not your crotch. When you land, you also turn your rear foot outward, protecting both knee and hip. When you land, you don't think about any of this. Your body reacts, like blinking.

This usually works.

I caught my landing, fingers splayed, palms soft and cupped for cushion. I heard *snap* before I felt my knee hit wood. My hip crunched. My body crumbled onto herself and I knew before I moved, I'd failed to turn my foot. It took two months for my hip-to-rib bruising to fade. It took daily physical therapy to repair torn muscle and tendon and, still, today, my hip lags—loose, lax, unstable.

I didn't know I was pregnant. Didn't know my baby-seed had found his way into my womb. My body failed to show normal prenatal symptoms—weight gain, morning sickness, devouring jars of pickles. Instead, she tired. This tiredness impacted my training. My routine launched at five am with hyper-flexibility drills and lasted until midnight choreography runs. Six days a week, no matter. If you knew me then, you'd know of my Olympic-level worry ability. So when my exhaustion hit, I thought, *Terminal*.

Thank goodness, my first response when told, *You're pregnant*.

Then, *I'm not going to die*.

Then, *I can stop*.

I didn't know that I wanted to stop, but, here, my body knew she needed a break. I barely recognized her—my body—as she slumped into relief.

By his eighth month in utero, my boy wearied, busted my waters and poured his body out.

That's not quite the way it went.

My waters seeped. I drove myself to Labor & Delivery. They failed to check my fluids and instead, sent me home, *Bed rest till term*. Over the next few hours, my contractions surged as fluid dripped down my thighs. I phoned L&D.

The on-call nurse said, *Come again if you need to.*

I padded my seat with towels and drove the 45-minutes back.

A different doctor evaluated, noted my blood pressure, 170 over 110, calmly said, *You're close to stroking* and *You're in labor* and, even calmer, *Who sent you home?*

Despite Richter-level contractions, my baby wouldn't come. More accurately, he couldn't. My cervix wouldn't move. Don't ask me why. Ask her. She clamped down at a two.

After eight hours, the doctor said, *He's distressed.*

I heard, *C-Section.*

Heard, *Epidural.*

Heard, *Don't push.*

Funny, all my body wanted was to push.

Did I mention my hip still hurt?

At only four pounds, he finally pushed himself into this world. He arrived with twisted hands, clubbed feet, and a defective heart. His circadian rhythm was off by a day or a decade. Unable to coordinate sucking, swallowing, and breathing because he couldn't push his tongue to the roof of his mouth. This meant he was unable to eat.

I thought, *He just needs a little training.*

Strength training meant one-arm push-ups with weights strapped to my back. Meant a 45-pound plate hanging from my waist while tricep-dipping or pull-upping. Meant adding more than my body was designed to hold.

Here, my baby is unable to perform the tiniest movement—pressing his tongue to the back of his gums, the place where his two front teeth would eventually puncture through. Now, I wonder why push-ups ever felt critical. Wonder why size zero became my drive. Here, my baby swims in preemie clothes—everything too large—incubator, diaper, sky.

Within days, we—the neonatal nurse and me—tricked my boy into "eating." We taped his feeding tube to my shoulder. We pinched it shut. We let my boy squawk with hunger then offered him my nipple. Though he couldn't latch, he found his way. As soon as his lips brushed my breast, we unpinched the tube, releasing his meal, a mixture of breast milk and formula.

Before his "feedings," I stretched his tongue. No. I stretched his frenulum, the tendon that ties the tongue to the floor of the mouth. I placed the end of my pinky against the tendon and pushed.

I also cried.

I remember holding those hyper splits during flexibility drills. Feet on five-inch blocks as I lowered my pelvis to the ground. I held this position for three minutes. When done, I physically inched my thighs back together.

With my hands.

Here, the same nurse teaches me how to change my son's diaper through the sterility of his incubator, my veined hands pushing through gloved openings. Plastic wall between babe and mom, between life and death. Here, nothing else matters.

Then, I believed my son lacked the ability to live. Believed I had to do the work of keeping his body alive. This is untrue. My boy pushed through and, over time, he surpassed those early medical predictions and limitations. Next week is his 40th surgery, his third or fourth one for his heart.

He tells me, *Let's get it done.*

And again, I cry. All along, he has held this trust in me, in the world. He knew, perhaps even before he arrived, that pushing comes with cost. If you push when you shouldn't, you might find yourself torn, lax, unstable. He understood this then. I am only learning this now, the way stars cluster with light and pulse without a single push. The way Earth keeps her circles without force.

Blurred

I couldn't find my baby.

Even though he slept beside my queen in a doll-sized bassinet. And even though I slept, if I slept, with one palm shrouding his tiny chest. I waited for the rise, barely detectable. Held my breath until after the fall. Who knew night held so much length, long after the umbilical cord is severed. After the womb empties.

Here, 2001, I'm 35. Here, my vision measures 20/400 in one eye, worse in the other. When I read the newspaper—old-school print—I hold it so near, it imprints ink, letters and images on my nose. My skin, a constant sheen of gray. Those news worthy leads, the world's mess pressing into me while I wrestle to release my own,

as if I could,

as if I knew this then.

Before bed, before swaddling, I sink-sponge bathe my boy, pulse-check his ankles, look for lack of blood-flow—sweat, vomit, unconsciousness. I move through post-surgery wound care in a subconscious way because we—my son and me—remain in a perpetual state of recovery. After, I read him stories while tube-feeding him. You know, infant care for a special-needs preemie. Once I tuck him in, I set my timer for our next round. Our two-hour increments. I keep him calm. I keep him contained. I secure all loose objects.

Some nights, finding my glasses takes a minute. A minute. How much can turn in under 60 seconds.

It matters little that he curls alongside me. Matters little that I've a night light. Matters even less that my hand still covers his chest. I wake in panic, believe him gone, believe him blue.

If only I didn't need glasses, I tell myself.

I try to sleep wearing them.

I try to sleep.

At three months, he stabilizes enough that, between his surgeries, I endure Lasik.

You remain awake for this procedure.

They press on your eye, distort your vision, ask, *Can you feel that?*

And you think you can because the pressure creates a blur.

You ask, *Press again?*

You offer a "thumbs up."

The smell hits first—pungent, ash, death. It takes a minute to know this as burning flesh. It takes another minute, perhaps longer, to understand this is your scent, your burning flesh. The laser pulses.

You tell your heart, *Align with this hum.*

You tell your mind, *Stop thinking of Nazi death camps.*

Before our walks, I roll my baby. First, I tuck dish towels next to his arms and legs, securing him, otherwise he'll slip through the stroller's leg holes and plummet to the cement. I re-notice the world with my new sight. We pass a once familiar house, though now, each brick is clearly outlined. Tree trunks reshape with textured bark. The leaves hold veins. There exists a new structure before me—concrete, mortar, toothpaste.

Here, my son is blind. I know, I didn't tell you. I didn't tell you because I didn't know this yet. Technically, he's visually impaired, his lenses blocked by bilateral centralized cataracts. This visual diagnosis will later confirm one more symptom, confirm he is a syndrome baby. Later, after I learn of his visual scarcity, our strolls evolve. We slow. We pause.

I brush his hand against that trunk, say, *Tree,* or *Bark,* or *Rough.*

Bathtimes shift too. I add words with touch: *Soft towels,* and *Warm water,* and *Splash.*

Moments become visual description. Every sound, an explanation. I turn off talk radio and the telly to not confuse his language development.

By my mid-forties, 2010, my vision dims to 20/40.

Still, I gain new sight.

• I open my then-husband's phone with a code I didn't know I knew. Read texts between him and someone he calls "Russian." He agrees to bring them more money at their next "meet."

• I hear my then-husband when he tells me, *I'll bury you.* I feel his words—in my throat, in my feet—like concrete holding me, pulling me into ocean.

(Maybe this isn't hearing, but believing.)

- I see my "friend" when she says, *You suffer because you don't believe in Jesus.*

- I find safe passage out of marriage and friendships, find a portal.

- My portal—writing and fetaling—returns me to my heart.
    I learn my truest sight was never lost.
    Recently, my eye doctor warned me, *You've swelling in nerve endings.*
    I don't ask, *Is this from too many black eyes?*
    I develop episcleritis, which feels like a migraine in the eye. I wear reading glasses, driving glasses, blue-tinted computer glasses. Last year, I lost peripheral in my right eye. (Cause unknown.) I didn't notice. My doctor tested and told me. The year before, I attended residency at the Hemingway House. My glasses broke on my face while I read the news from my laptop. I blamed Ernest.
    Here I ask, *What am I not seeing?*
    Can we ever know?
    I didn't tell you, I've worn glasses since fourth grade. Those thick-bottle black ones. Everyone called them BC (birth control). In high school, my glasses covered most of my face, like a squid. Later, I joined the military and they issued me BC frames. Funny, these frames are back. Everyone wears them. Mel Robbins. Robert Downey Jr. John Mayer. And me.
    Me.
    I should tell you, I hate needing glasses. Should tell you that sometimes I toss my glasses, squint my way through the world. After 60 minutes I suffer a headache, tell myself, *Take the help, old girl.*
    Maybe I'm uncomfortable without challenge.
    Maybe easy
        feels unearned.
            Feels
                like I'm a liability.
    Today, 2025, I easily find my baby, now 24, a grown man. He sleeps three rooms away. He wears glasses to bed. Our calico rests on his chest. From his door frame, I watch her—the cat—rise. Watch her fall. Her outline blurs into the backdrop—

indigo moonlight pouring through his window. From outside, wind whooshes our chimes. And I, I lean against the wall, lean into my son's rhythm. I stay this way longer than a minute. Longer. I close my eyes, breathe, and welcome the night.

When Fireflies Scatter

It must've been the Fourth because the 12-gauge leaned in the crook, a corner in the space we called our dining room. It was just a kitchen—one square Formica table with a bowl of sugar in the center and four, maybe five stiff-cushioned metal chairs tucked tight. You could extend your arm and touch the stove on one side, the fridge on the other. This year—they tell me—will be my year to blast shells to sky and stars, to aim for the moon. This year, at midnight, I'll rip off one, maybe three shells from Daddy's shotgun.

We—my bio brother, my fostered and adopted siblings, some kid named Dennis who lives one block over, and me—play outside till ten. We start with ghosts in the graveyard. We always start with the ghosts. Here, they catch me first because I refuse to hide. I refuse to hide because our yard holds one tree. I refuse to hide because this tree—a 20-foot pine—houses webs, ticks, and spiders. I know these critters will weave into my hair, nest, and make babies. Or worse, find their way into my pores, maybe eat me alive from the inside out. I wish for a weeping willow, like the Hetricks', a tree with canopy.

This is the mid-70s. I'm in fourth or fifth grade and patriotism is at a high. We wear red, white, and blue tees, shoes, headbands. We enter the bicentennial with pride. We love old Abe and think fondly of Washington's wooden teeth. Teachers avoid the "other" history—slaves, colonialism, and napalm. Instead, we create stars and stripes from everything—Styrofoam balls, papier-mâché, brown paper lunch bags—which we later turn into Uncle Sam puppets.

I'm nine or ten. This is the first time I shoot a gun, but not the first time I've held one. I wish I could tell you specifics. I can tell you what I remember. I remember the cherry-almond scent of Jergens hand lotion. I remember the glass Skippy jar slipping and shattering. I remember Irene, a beautiful teenage girl and her older brother, Elias, who my parents fostered. They lived with us just under a year. I remember Irene's, *No*, when Daddy handed her the gun.

As midnight nears, we circle, center in the kitchen, nine, maybe ten of us.

You need to learn how to protect yourself, young lady, Daddy says.

Irene shakes her head. Her eyes well. I lean into the corner, nodding small to show support. We—my adopted sister, Tina, Irene, and me—share a room. When Irene first moved in, she taught me how to French braid, not just hair, but also loaves of bread.

You move three pieces, one over the other, again and again. Like us, she said, *three sisters*. Her voice, soft like butter. Her hands laced everything with slow, meticulous care.

Here, Cedar Lake, Indiana, and nearing midnight, Irene snatches the gun from Daddy, rests the butt on her shoulder, aims it straight. At him. She looks down the gun. Something inside me rises—glee, hope, a definite *Yes*. Daddy pushes the muzzle aside and laughs.

You forgot who you're dealing with, girl, he says.

He yanks the gun from her and hands it to me.

Your turn, Becki.

He offers no warnings, no safety tips, no goggles. Only the gun.

I grab the weapon, the most power given to me at this tender age. My face heats, my hands wet with sweat. I walk outside, letting the screen door squeal shut. The sky, moonless, tenderly lit by the sprinkles of fireflies. I nestle the metal into my shoulder. I think of that time Irene sat on our bed—two girls facing one another.

She asked in the softest way, *Did he get you, too?*

I only nodded then.

I only nodded for years after.

I look into the night, and all that blackness, and I squeeze. I squeeze that trigger. I squeeze and blast, scattering only fireflies and perhaps one lone widow hidden in the needles of our pine.

War Zoning with a Toddler on My Back

I hope I never forget the way we played, especially Nerf gun wars. The way you shared your birthday—year after year—with Zach, your older, disabled brother. And the way you let him call you *Baby* till the third grade. We all knew he meant it affectionately. You, younger than he. You, taller and stronger and passing him by in life skills and wit.

We sit at our table, negotiating party locations, circa 2012.

Chucky Cheese, Zach shouts.

That's for little kids, you say.

The zoo, Zach offers.

We live in a zoo, you say.

Julian, your toddler brother, tosses a small stuffed elephant from his highchair just so I'll pick it up. You beat me to it, grab the animal, and stomp around the kitchen, arm straight out like a trumpet. Julian claps. Zach sinks into a thinking face and I'm sure he's working hard to guess the perfect place for a party with his big-little brother.

Do you remember Zach in a cape no matter the season?

You both love light sabers and Nerf guns, I say. *What if we plan a theme like that?*

You stop acting like an elephant, morph back to boy, sit and smile. I grin, too, happy to get it right.

Can we have pizza? you ask.

Julian claps, throws his elephant further.

I nod.

Can we have a Batman cake? Zach says.

Sure, Buddy, you tell him.

And right then, I hope I never forget your generous ways with him.

Your and Zach's birthdays are five days apart. When you were born, Zach wanted only to hold you. He couldn't talk yet—almost two—but he continuously signed, *Baby,* and *Love,* and *Me Want* during my entire pregnancy with you. At birth, you weighed over eight pounds, only a pound and a half smaller than toddler Zach. I have so many pictures from this time. You resting in Zach's lap, Zach's head barely peeking around. You and Zach, side by side on your bellies, facing the camera, your chubby hands holding your chins. And later, you and Zach, wearing only underwear, your body painted orange, Zach's green. Both of you flexing tiny boy muscles, posing like two Hulks.

For this birthday celebration, we meet your friends at The War Zone in Meridian, Idaho. First, Nerf gun training, a mix of safety instructions and gathering gear—vests, weapons, ammunition. The room steams with the excitement of youth; young boy body odor mixed with talc and breakfast bacon burps. All of you, ready to battle, ready to win.

You'll be teamed with others already out there, the instructor says, and, *Keep your goggles on*, and, *If you get hit, be honest or we'll tap you out.*

We nod—your friends, Zach, you, and me.

Can my brother be on my team? you ask.

And I make another note, *Remember that smile spreading 'cross Zach's face.*

The other parents stay behind, sit in the lobby, wait for pre-ordered pizzas, and sip sodas while guarding our Batman fondanted cake.

We move room by room much like the way I decontaminated during chemical warfare training. Back then, mid-1980s at RAF Upper Heyford, we wore our charcoal suits and rubber boots over Air Force uniforms as we shuffled through a series of chambers. The heavy airlock door held air so stale we knew it hadn't been changed in years, like the filters in our gas masks. Still today, the smell of hot tar and fresh tires brings a gag. Our boots splashed through invisible waters as we passed filtration and ventilation equipment, certain this would save us from the ill effects of nerve agents and nukes.

I remember the way we stepped into the war zone. In the military, we kicked up sand and kept our canteen sips small. Just in case. Here, we walk through a door, like a portal, out of the party and into a black-lit obstacle course. Julian squeezes the back of my leg as I squat low, push the goggles higher on my nose and

Zach and you disappear.

I tuck,
    roll,
        and dive.

I take down big men and small children. I barrel roll behind a Styrofoam wall, *Nailed*, I whisper, hitting them—the enemy—in the neck, the shoulder, the ear lobe. All the while, Julian digs his fingers into my flesh, his arms wrapped tight around my neck like a monkey. Midpoint, I'd forgotten that I hoisted him. Another midpoint and I'd forgotten I packed him on my back as I army crawled over mats, Nerf bullets spraying overhead.

Mamma, Julian whispers.

Shhhhhh. We cannot risk detection.

Few men still stand. I count six, but I feel seven.

                        Bam. Bam. Bam.

I take out three. Direct forehead hits.

                My goggles fog,

                my mascara drips,

                my body crusts with crystalized sweat.

Slowly, I realize….

                you and Zach…

                  and your birthday party friends…

                          are no longer in the war zone,

                              no longer in my visual field.

We—Julian and me—weave our way out of war and into the lobby.

I pull my goggles up over my damp hair, wipe wetness from my face. I pry Julian's grip, but only to loosen. The parents of the party pause, mouths agape. They glare at me. Messy me. Everyone is seated, chomping pizza, and you, you don't miss a beat.

Welcome back, Mom.

The next year when the first crocus shows,

when your birthdays surface,

when I ask,

Would you like to share your day again?

Yes, you say.

Another Nerf gun war?

Uhm, Mom, that's kinda your thing.

I'm the Deadliest

When his karate instructor shouts, *Fear nothing*, my son responds—army-style—*Sorry Sir*, then breaks the chunk of pine with the side of his hand.
He stands taller.
He bows.
He adds, *I fear my mother.*
We laugh.
We know his fear is not of me. We understand he fears for others, for those who bring my fierceness forward. He knows the ones who've damaged me (and him).
Later, we—my sons and me—Nerf-gun war during winter holidays. We goggle up. I nab two assault rifles. When they jam, I dash back to our garage, our "armory." I pack two pistols, weave my way up the stairs, back against the wall, trigger finger long and ready. I sense my son, pop up, hit him between the eyes.
Gotcha! I shout.
I step over dogs. When I say, *Dogs*, I mean four 144-lb Newfoundlands who transform into a wall, a forest, a mountain. I reach the top, belly to the ground, army crawl to the chair, re-pop and…our Newfies surround, hold me down, hold me under, slobber me in kisses.
I laugh, *Why me? I'm the smallest.*

*

Some say, *It's wise to slow your anger.*
I say, *Let anger beast herself.*
We've forgotten that anger acts as a bodyguard for hurt. We hurt from destruction. Destruction cast upon us. Destruction we cast upon ourselves or, worse, destruction to which we bear witness. Like that lone teen bludgeoned to death. To death. In a high school bathroom.
I say, *If I meet those bludgeoners, I hope they smell my danger.*
Hope they feel my angst crawl along their nape, claw their throat. Much like their fist.

Their fist.

Even later, I convince a friend to buy bamboo sheets.

Rid toxic body fluids out of those other, lesser threads, I say. *Burn 'em.*

And she does. She burns, baby, burns. She might think me untamed, tameless, untrainable because I'm clear. It looks like I know what I want. Really, I know what I don't want.

Typically, I respond, *I got it myself.*

You might think bamboo pokey, but when you snap those sheets wide to spread atop your bed, they clap. As if they approve of you.

As if they tell you, *Go ahead, indulge.*

They cost less than high-count threads. Cheaper in money-hours and blood-calloused fingertips. The price others pay for our comfort. The cost of a good night's sleep. The cost of a good night.

I wish I were bamboo, able to bend under pressure, to move with storm, to stand still after.

*

After I "kill" my son in our family Nerf-gun battle, he sits, criss-cross on the floor, elbows propped on our hand-built Lego table. This table stretches twelve by eight feet. This table is cut from pine and stained in walnut, with a lid that weighs nearly 50 pounds. Inside, we glued a light and lined the interior with baseplates. We build cities, war plans, and sometimes, ice-cream parlors. Right now, this table acts as our enemy holding tank. My son rubs the now-reddened spot on his forehead.

You're the deadliest, he says.

Maybe I am.

I'll tell you, *I'm tangled and lush.*

Tell you, *I'm some wild outback landscape built of fire and spit.*

I'm rainforest damp, morning-kiss dewed. You know me by my muskiness. Also, by my spark. My oaky scent drifts ahead of me, like a decent reputation. Despite my heavy—my heavy heart—I rise, lighter than lashes, than breath, than sheer-webbed autumn leaves who barely hang on. I take flight, ride the wind in a blink.

*

Before all of this, 1986, I harness into an F-111. The pilot pushes four Gs and my face spreads. I swear my nose touches my ears. I worry about wrinkles, though I'm only 20. Later, in my 30s, I climb into a hot air balloon and float the Idaho foothills. Below us, matchbox-sized cars move like slow ants along a winding trail. They grow smaller till there is but a ribbon through the rifts. The continuous yapping of backyard dogs reaches me. The autos stay silent. No rev. No squealing brakes. No afterfires.

I think, *Dogs must be the only ones who can talk to angels.*
I believe this.
I believe this still.
I flutter over those hills, basket rocking in unseen breeze. The barking reminds me of the way bamboo trees bang into one another in storm, their melody like maracas.

I tell myself, *Here I sit in the palm of the Divine, and she's holding me.*

I'm sunrise built of lavender and mango.
I'm everything you think I'm not.
And more.

*

Sometimes, when they—my son and his friends—gather out front, I harness myself with Nerf guns, ammo, and a toothpick. I circle the tires, pop over the hood, roll, and *Splat! Splat!* Two down. Four to go. *Pay attention,* I shout over my shoulder, retreating to our house. They—the neighbor boys—love my unpredictability. Me? I'm just trying to remain tuned, polished, war-ready.

I'm more like oak, I'll tell you.

At least as a mom. I grow slowly. I wish to live long. I tend my thick trunk and thicker skin. I often save my leaves 'til spring. I'm strong and glean a straight grain. I need full sun and well-drained soil. I rarely bend. I rarely break, as well. You might hear my whisper in the night-wind as you quiet.

I say, *You got this.*
Perhaps I say this for me, only me, my mantra, my storm song.
I got this.
I got this.
I got this myself.

We Leave Our Signature in Cement

At the wall, I'm 23, and squished between my American boyfriend and a German. We're surrounded with nationality, as if the entire world arrived just to scratch a piece of history. We scratch Berlin's barrier mortared from flesh and filament. We scratch away stone stories. Scratch more than our hands can carry. Scratch one chunk, and then another and another, greedy to hold place, hold a moment.

Two years later, we sleep in rows in tent city. We tell ourselves we're providing comfort to Kurdish refugees. Tell ourselves that dropping parcels on the mountaintop makes a difference.

Tell ourselves, *It's ok,* when those same crates land on the very humans we tell ourselves we're saving.

Tell ourselves, *Our presence matters.*

Near the mountain, I press myself into the temporary city built from sand and tin. I press the heels of my hands into the boy's chest. I press two inches deep, and count—one and two and three and four. I press while sweat drips from brow to breast, splattering the backs of my hands.

I press and whisper, *Comeoncomeoncomeon.*

We build a city within our built cities. We name it Arkham City Hall. We build this city, yet another tent, to house security police. We keep our humor as we build. We laugh aloud while we build. We wipe our snot with the backs of our hands sand-gritted from all our building. We keep building.

Packed over time and beneath my nails lives a city curated from skin and flesh. Flesh from men who took me without permission. Flesh of men who, while taking me, took more than my body held. Flesh of commanders, strangers, lovers, bosses, fathers. Flesh then, but now dead. Dead skin. Flesh—dead or not—still lives in my nail bed city. Flesh beneath my nail beds. Flesh in my bed of nails. Flesh in my bed.

My heart-city navigates much like London—tube travel, sushi on the run, Jack the Ripper walking tours, black death, and Andrew Lloyd Weber. This, my city-beat set somewhere between "Memory" and "Time to Say Goodbye." This, my farewell to the body cities I never could love—my ass and abs and nose.

This, my wish for a city of romance within me, like Aix-en-Provence. This heart-city still beats, despite man's greatest effort to silence her.

Ten years after Berlin, I'm 33, spread like a snow angel on a cement floor. 33 and I'm in a warehouse in the middle of Boise, Idaho. 33 and I'm in the center of a rave, holding hands with a girl I don't know. 33 and all I want is to protect this stranger-girl whom I call *Pigtails*. 33 and I'm in bell-bottom hip-huggers and a cut-off tank and Pigtails wears athletic knee highs with heels. 33 and I stay still, imprinting my body, leaving my signature in that cement like the outline of a murder scene.

Between Berlin and Pigtails and the boy, the boy, the boy, I visit Auschwitz and the Eagle's Nest, though not on the same day or month or year. How wrong to stand in the heart of those chambers. Wrong to witness atrocity's aftermath. Wrong, after, to paint my eyes with prettier places—Dover's White Cliffs, Mozart's bedroom, Beatles' Strawberry Fields.

When night descends, my mind-city takes over, takes cover, takes. I wrestle memories like an enemy. I wrestle locks and bolts as I try to seal myself into safety. I wrestle my weighted blanket. I wrestle shadows flickering from the soft light of my small lamp. I wrestle shadow-men shaped into soldiers and refugees and everyone I ever failed. I wrestle the stink of boss-breath and Pigtails' sweat still on my palm and the boy, the boy whose chest I pressed and pressed and, despite my compressing he didn't make it.

I'm a composition of cities, most of whom have visited me. I'm framed and constructed and now, I am trying to record my city, myself. If only I could splatter a bit of gold and sun back into the world. Re-coat cement, curate glass stained so beautiful and in every hue. Create a self-portrait of me and you and her and him
                      and them
                                  and us.

RePrints for a Poet

I once read that if you lie on your bed upside down, your brain reorganizes earlier sleep portraits. When I say, *Upside down*, I don't mean bat-like. I mean head towards the foot of your bed, feet towards the headboard. Some of us sleep one third of our lives. Perhaps we should reconsider sleep direction. Even those who are not great sleepers. I'm not. I nap. I spurt-rest.

When I lie this way, head at my footboard, feet at my head, I wear a pink eye mask that reads *Sweet Dreams* in black letters. She blocks light. She tricks my mind into night-breath. She fools my body with hope: maybe this is the night I'll heal. If only a little.

When I wake, no matter the time, I pad through the house shoeless, check window locks, door locks. *Are there ever enough locks?* I used to blame my ex for my nervousness. Then I blamed his hitman. Later, I blamed the military. Even later, I'll blame the one person responsible for all my hang-ups: my mother.

One should always blame one's mother.

To avoid lock security illusion, I read. I read because I stopped watching news. I stopped watching news the same time I stopped sleeping right-side up, tits facing the heavens, scalp against my headboard. I stopped news-watching while sitting dispatch in Turkey witnessing CNN and BBC and another local station report on the Gulf War. They each told a different tale. My military briefings matched none of their stories. Our debriefings matched none of our briefings. My on-foot combat boot experience— handing food to Kurdish refugees—matched nothing. Even now as I read and reread old orders, articles, and documents, they—the superiors—failed to mention the way we left them—the refugees. Left them to die.

Did I tell you, *I'm a poet?*

Tell you, *I wonder where truth lies?*

Once, I tried to sleep sideways. Another time, I slept diagonally. And when I slept in these positions, I woke disoriented, feet tied and tangled in sheets, pulse thumping near my brows.

I sleep with a body pillow. I named him Herman. I sleep with a neck roll, lumbar support, and an extra wedge between my knees. I sleep curled, like a hedgehog, and sprawled, like a scattered newspaper.

I tell myself, *Avoid watching currency*—those war-torn bodies—*and if you can mask yourself from blood and bone, you just might sleep.*

Or un-capture those missing child images. If only I could unthink those predator kid-nappers with their lost puppy tricks. Un-see the starving populations, bellies distended, eyes sinking and bulging at once.

I've forgotten.

I'm a poet. I read in images.

Maybe I started sleeping upside-down after that leveraged sex, that time I hooked my feet beneath my headboard, my lover kneeling between my thighs, holding my wrists above me. I orgasmed so hard that I nearly blacked out. Perhaps that near-blacking induced my brain into believing that this is the way to fall into sleep. The way to circumvent those snapshots.

But I'm a poet. I write in images.

Did I tell you, *I need images?*

It makes sense. I need images to sleep. Not those bleed-to-lead newsreels. I need a fresh layer. I need to uncurl my brain. I need a blank canvas. I need memory to repaint herself with acrylics or oils or butterscotch pudding, allowing ancestral bruising—the blacks, the blues—to repurpose as foundation. If only I could drag a brush through my mind and give one new image permission to exist.

Before I sleep, I offer my worries to a little box filled with four tiny people. I gift a concern to each person. I write the remaining in my journal.

I tell Alexa, *Play ocean sounds.*

I breathe in through my nose. I release my tongue from the roof of my mouth. I unclench my teeth, unfist my hands. I invert myself, prop and position my body. My lips move, like prayer.

I chant for sleep, plea for relief, mask [and unmask] upside down in my bed. I wait for my rise—bile and brew and dawn—rewriting memories until I surrender, roll out, slip into slippers, check locks and toast a bagel.

I pour my thoughts—pen to page—tell myself, *This will heal what the body holds.*

Sometimes, instead, the words pour moreandmoreandmore back into my body. Until my ink runs dry. I write until my ink dries.

I write.

I write in images.

I'm a poet.

Writing "Me"

I wrote nonfiction in third person. I know, not the usual way to share narrative.

I told myself, *This approach! A style all my own.*

At the time, 2012, all my stories held a "she" instead of a "me" perspective.

In workshop, others processed my material as if it were fabricated. Feedback included, *She would never do that* or *Nope* or *Not believable.*

They—the other writers—offered advice, like, *What if she felt bad about lying, you know, create more tension?*

Or, *Maybe she fights back so she doesn't get raped but comes close.*

Those sessions hit like a blend of lecture, counseling, and skydiving. Of course, I wish my character (me) had responded to life in a more heroic way. Wish my character (me) could have acted honorably. Wish my character (me) would quit hibernating.

Don't we all?

Still, my third-person approach proved successful. When I tell you, *Successful,* I don't mean publication or recognition or any external validation. I mean that I discovered—quite accidentally—that through the use of third person, I could pen my most vulnerable history—the events that damaged me, that changed me, that shamed me. Writing in third person meant I could write my life as if writing about someone else. With this approach, I turned raw, juicy, willing to commit to truth. This formula meant less editing because I remained detached, me from my own story. Me from me.

2017, during my first residency at Sierra Nevada's MFA program, I wanted to read one of these dangerous pieces at open mike. I selected a section from a larger body of work-in-progress. The piece was based on a prompt from the poem, "If These Old Walls Could Talk," often used in a therapeutic setting. This excerpt distanced itself from me, not just through third person, but also through the perspective of my childhood bedroom walls. I'd shared the essay with my mentor before the reading.

Why third person? she asked.

It's clever, isn't it? I said.

Well, it does keep you safe, she said, and added, *But, this removes you, not only from your own story, but from the reader. Your material might be too hard to do this but maybe try to retell it in first person.*

Then she asked about those walls. If I stayed behind walls, I created even more space between me and my own story. Between me and you.

I edited the piece on and off between coursework. That revision—one page—brought me to my barren bathroom floor, alone in my dorm room.

I thought, *I'll head to the common area to work.*

I gathered my pages, my pen, my courage and sat outside with two, maybe three, other students. We worked in silence, some in headphones, others tuned in with ancient Earth-hum. The Nevada sky melted from blue into a deep purple, like royalty. I glanced from my pain just as a bear, maybe fifteen feet away, walked through.

I mouthed, *Bear. Bear.*

I pointed. One of the students turned. Both of us gape-mouthed. Two cubs pranced behind that mamma. We knew not to move. Not to blink. Not to breathe.

In that stillness I remember thinking, *Protecting one's children need not be brutal. It can be simple. It can mean 'Presence.'*

As I write this, I'm also reminded that writing, even with a group of creative spirits and Mother Nature herself, will always stay a solo flight. I'm reminded, *My interpretation of that bear is unique.* The way I capture narrative will be not only through my eyes and memories, but must also include my heart. That night I knew I needed to reconnect my own story to me. I needed to own my story. I needed my story.

I cried alone in my room before that open mike as I tried to read my single page aloud to my reflection. I couldn't get through the words as me, as I. How could I read it in front of a room full of writers, many of them published authors and professors?

I coaxed myself, *Do this. Do this one thing.*

And I believed—then and still—if I could read this one page aloud completely as myself, I could do anything. I'm a public speaker, a motivational coach, a radio show host. I was Mrs. Idaho, a television show host, a world-level performance athlete. I rarely shy from public attention. Still, when my turn to speak arrived, my legs shook. My voice fractured. What trickled out of me was not my own sound. At least not one that I recognized. I cried. I cried at that podium. I cried for my history. I cried for me, for my adopted sister, for everyone who ever endured sexual assault. Here, finally, I felt. Something. I had no idea that I'd numbed myself most of my 50-plus years.

For the first time in my life, my story mattered. Here, I understood. It matters not if my prose and poems ever enter the world. Writing will change me, alter my course, reshape the arc of my own narrative.

A Little Letter from an AI Rebutter

I am an AI Rebutter.
I am a Long-Hand-Writer Endorser.
I pen pages each morning in a journal, jot a list of tasks to (almost) complete, scaffold essays and poems across composition notebooks. In separate journals, I copy beautiful lines from artists I love, wishing to transfer talent by osmosis.
For me, magic begins within this first planting.
I lean into an unfolding. Instead of writing towards an idea or theme or popular topic, I follow the words where they lead. It is from this space in my first drafts that I discover seedlings. Tiny sprouts. Sometimes one piece feels as though it could be in conversation with a piece of work I developed earlier. Other times, I might recognize the start of a poem. I rarely see the entire piece, near completion, in that first long-handwritten scratch. And when I do, I most likely have been working out that essay or poem in my head and heart for some time. Perhaps decades.
From these drafts, I transfer work out of my notebooks and into my computer. I sort them, temporarily name them, file them, hope to return and flush them out and into some semblance of literary art. Some of them make it out alive. Many appear dormant. They are not. These are transplanted seeds now contained and, in their incubation, like a compost-covered perennial, they rest until ready to bloom.
Every artist holds a process of their own. This is mine. And this early delicate care is critical for my art. This is the beginning. The revision and the polishing—the places I thin fruit and prune or add nutrients—come much later. THAT process requires highlighters and research and sitting with my art as if I'm with an old friend.
The argument I've heard from my writer-friends who use AI seems reasonable. One friend shares that she uses AI to get the first draft down and save time. And I think, *Oh! She wants quantity. She's writing for a page number, not the process of art.* Another writer explains that AI works with her initial idea and helps expand her thoughts into a draft that is further along, something she can begin editing. And I think, *Ok, she's looking for a shortcut.*

I know I sound judgy and each writer has the right to produce a product for the world to enjoy by whatever means.

And yes, I've heard the AI argument: *Well, I built the foundation, which is my idea, with a new medium—the computer. And from there I revise. And, isn't true art in the revision?*

I couldn't agree more. As we polish, we begin to see the shape, the storyline, the narrative arc, the angel in the stone. Someone somewhere taught me this same concept, *Art is in the revision.*

I repeat this to my writing students. I say this aloud to myself.

Yet when I hear this phrase resurrected in the context of an AI defense, it feels as if my child is misquoting me.

If you extend the argument that generative AI is still your work, your heart-art, and working with a draft generated for you is still your art, then I believe you've lost your artist's way.

If you share your idea with another writer and paid that writer to write your first draft, yet you polish the draft, are you still the artist?

Isn't this now a collaborative project?

Perhaps your name is on the byline, but the piece is ghostwritten.

Aren't you simply editing AI's work?

My worry for future artists is their need for instant gratification. Our society pressures this fast-paced finishing, pushing artists to produce more and produce as quickly as possible. I think we lose something special in our hyper-production mentality. It's the difference between delicately placing a spotless ladybug on your rose bush, allowing her to do her job, versus spraying with chemicals that harm us—you, me, our soil, our air—to quickly rid the buds of aphids.

We're losing the slow-infusing, flowering benefits of blooming. The investment of curation has been replaced. We've the cut-and-pasted Happy Holiday text message sent to the masses instead of our soft, curly strokes of the handwritten card. We've lost the homemade bread aroma, the gathering at a table for a game, the random phone call, the old-fashioned family portraits.

Time is our greatest commodity. The way we use time defines us. This sets our tone, our day, our hearts. Will we notice the dew of grass beneath our feet? Will we stop and smell the roses…or anything? The micro moments are where we live and absorb the world. The pause is often the loudest note in a song. The space between the first longhand in an under- or over-written draft becomes the pulse of the poem.

    I want the entire art experience. I want this whether I'm the artist or the audience. I want to feel the duende in the flamenco, the fire in the cello, the tears in the writer. I want to feel this as I create—one slow step to the next. This intentional early movement helps me discover me, helps me understand the way I'm ingesting the world. Helps me.

When a Bear Isn't Mentioned in Your Horoscope

It's summer, 2023, and I take to the Hemingway House. I stand in the center, the large glass doors accordioned open as I run my fingers along the spines of books rowed on shelves, the work of earlier residents. I've read them all. Own their catalogs. Wolff. Houston. Strayed. Urrea. I pull *The House of Broken Angels*, the pages worn and fat from use. I press the cover—smooth and cool—to my cheek, and I swear cedar or birch lingers.

How did I get here? I might've said this aloud.

I'm staying for a mini writing residency here in Ketchum, Idaho, atop mountains, near river, nearer sky.

All to myself.

All by myself.

Here, this morning, I browse my 2025 horoscope forecast, *The year will challenge and reward you in equal measure.*

Man, they play it safe, I think.

*

Here, this morning, in Star, Idaho, I'm alone in my office, but not really. My 16-year-old preps his second Dungeons & Dragons session for the week, which involves as much food as thought. Before settling in with my keyboard and coffee, I dash to Albertsons, hair frazzled from a night of unsleep, my Spider-man pajamas barely hidden beneath my parka. I fill my cart with frozen pizzas, sodas, and chips. It's eight am. Other half-awake shoppers avert their eyes and I'm sure they wonder if I've forgotten, *I'm in public.*

Besides my Hemingway House Stay, I can't remember my last aloneness. I often feel alone, despite my surround-sound clatter of Newfoundland love and man-cub angst.

That stay at the Hemingway House held little variation from my normal life, if you can call any life "normal." I organize stations, much like an obstacle course, most likely akin to my 2025 forecasted existence: 1) A stack of journals awaiting tabbing, labeling, indexing. 2) A yoga mat. 3) Next to the soft leather chair, a pile of to-be-reads, which I didn't read. 4) In a separate room, my computer. 5) Near the bed—a fig candle, prayer book, journal, and a Sharpie S-Gel with a fine point.

Within my stations, I frantically move, frenzying to finish something, anything, only to begin another. I do this at Hemingway's home. I do this in Star. I do this every morning. I did this 20 years ago and if you knew me then, you'd have heard my nice ex-but-now-dead husband, *You're always so busy. We just don't know what you're busy doing.*

Doing.

I'm a Doing-Human, not a Being-Human.

That stay with Hemingway, I was neither—Doing nor Being—I was Trying.

I might be a Trying-Human.

This is my way, whether in the presence of Hemingway—well, his ghost—or alone.

I tried.

I try.

The quiet during my Hemingway Stay sounds so loud that it pains me.

Not true.

There is little quiet. My feet *slap* 'cross the cement floors. My breath whistles like windstorm. *Could that kettle squeal any slower?* I feel her rise, build, then break.

With every blink, my ears crackle—a sound I failed to notice before and here, at the House, I wonder, *How long has this been going on?*

My first night during my Hemingway Stay, I wake. No. I almost-wake or not-wake. My bedding lifts high above me. I lie motionless, voiceless, in a state of dream paralysis. I fight through my frozen, near-death moment and jump from bed. I shove my carefully laid-out stations into duffles.

I drop my bags and slide open the glass door.

I'm out of here, I say, voice shaking, air cold enough to see my breath.

Outside, the night holds a blackness so heavy my breath disappears. So does my ear-crackle. I hold my hand in front of my face and cannot see it. Instead, I picture a bear, perhaps inches away, steam misting off his fur.

Oh, I say, and, *It's you.* I somehow recognize Hemingway.

I do not flee because the potential bear between my car and me scares me more than some angsty ghost.

Listen, I say. *I don't want to be afraid of you. Can you just help me?*

*

This morning, sometime in 2025, we—Hem and me—know that my own ghost is far angstier than any other.

If I look up my horoscope from July 2023, during my Hemingway Stay, I find: *This is a month of further transformational intensity, involving a strong spiritual element in what you do out in the world, including all aspects of your creativity.*

This morning, I wonder if I paid enough attention then.

I wonder if my effort during my Hemingway Stay predicted who I am today.

Wonder what my effort today will curate for my future self.

I believed, at the end my Hemingway Stay, I would feel myself a true artist, a real writer. I imagined returning home, setting aside my distractions and disabilities, doubling down, pulling up my socks, wiping my nose.

Instead, I sink into life-demands—juggling family and obligations.

Most mornings I say, *I'm afraid,* though I'm not sure what I fear.

I often wake, even when I'm not asleep, with the sense I'm still in some state of dream paralysis. Me, frozen. Me, with my own ghost.

Oh, I say.

It's not just my ghost. I can still smell that bear and he's clean. Like fresh soil I just turned in my backyard garden.

Oh, I say, and, *Playing safe equates to a bear devouring me.*

I need to sit with my ghost. Open her wound. Let her bleed clean through. I need to write what I'm terrified to tell you. Mess up my tidy creative stations.

It is time.

Time for me to tell myself, *I don't want to be afraid.*

WaPo Horoscope—Cancer, Sept 28th, 2024

They advise, *Be a passive viewer today.*

When done writing this, I'll teach my workshop, *Untangling the Difficult Narrative.* Usually in these gatherings, there are tears, there are few men, there are stories delicately unpacked. Stories bodies have carried through ancestral sands.

They tell us, *Be an active listener.*

Most of us need this. Distractions thrive. Our minds wander. Lips move before we thoroughly hear another's rant. Or song.

I don't know how to do either—passively view, actively listen.

They advise, *Clear your schedule today.*

I only allow this when ill or post-surgery. It never feels like a choice. Never feels quite right letting others down, saying, *No,* or, *I'm sorry.* Again. Especially without reason. Do people do this? Simply clear their schedule. I wonder what I would do with an entire day absent of obligation, expectation. How would I manage myself? I fear I'll stay in bed. Fear I'll sleep and it will feel so wonderful that I'll empty the rest of my year, the rest of my life. Fear I will take up oxygen, hold my breath, and not give anything back.

I don't know how to quiet my schedule and be with only me. I don't know how to not "do" life.

They advise, *Let your mind wander.*

And I think, *Does my mind do anything but?*

In a call last night, my close friend of 25 years asked, *Do you think I'm ADD?*

Yes, I said, and, *Aren't we all?*

I taught my brain to work in spurts. I weave through revisions, a flash essay collection, nothing over 1000 words. I can't seem to write past that number.

Somewhere I read that humans in Western culture can't commit to more than 1000 words. 1000 seconds. To push past this limit, I began training my brain. *Focus-schooling,* I call it. I'm at ten minutes in a row while painting or reading or studying. It took three months to arrive here.

I tell myself, *The brain is a muscle.*

Tell myself, *Train it.*

Tell myself, *Sweat your way to one hour.*

Can you imagine sitting with a luscious book for one hour? All those delicious minutes in a row?

I will not wander.

I will not wander with my mind.

I will mind my wander.

They advise, *Today is the day to toss out the rule book.*

I wonder which rule book I should toss. Certainly not the driving one. That three-inch yellow line painted down the center of the road keeps you on your side, me on mine. Prevents us from bashing head-on at an impact twice our speed and weight. Certainly I shouldn't toss my cookbooks. If you omit sugar, nothing browns. There are rules to follow, like wearing pants outside my home or filling my tank when low. Or brushing my teeth, more beneficial for you than me. I buckle my seatbelt in the garage. Look behind before backing up. Look again, just in case.

They advise, *Allow for life's capricious nature*, and I think, *Don't I do this all the time?*

How unreliable and volatile the world is. California caught fire. Dead hostages are returned. Trump has defunded, rescinded defunding, tariffed, and deported. The second atmospheric river weaves her way 'cross California. And there's the fickle way we live with other beings who keep us guessing no matter. There are moods and flavors and needs, some that are not your own. And all these random connections, like that time your 16-year-old says, *Sometimes all we have in common is murders and music.* You don't want him to be right. Still, you beg him to watch one more *True Detective* episode, though it's eleven pm and he has school the next day. You ask anyway. After midnight, you shower, head to bed with a wet head because blow-drying feels like too much. Once the last pup nuzzles in, you wonder, *Who parents whom? Whose advice should we follow?* Then you doom-scroll Instagram reels for another hour. Your eyes burn and your heart slows and you may or may not flip off your lamp, but you will remind Alexa, *Play ocean waves.* And here, you listen…intently hearing the whispers, the wisdom some AI-generated sound machine created. You wonder about your horoscope for the next day. You remember, *It's the next day.* You stretch wide 'cross your bed, tell your body, *Pretend you're a dune.* You pretend the sun kisses your skin. Pretend that all is well.

Boosters

When you're young, in the '70s, they booster you. You'll take it in your shoulder, most likely because they line you up with others just like you. They line you in the hall at school.

They ask, *Right or left*, and you opt for left because you favor your right.

No one tells you what the injection holds. No one tells you why you need it. This is a time you do as you're told. A time kids are seen, not heard. A time you climb to the gym ceiling on a knotted rope with only a thin blue mat 30 feet below to catch you when you lose your grip. Because you will. Lose your grip. You live with risk. You think yourself tough. You don't know better. You don't know much.

Later, you'll learn they inoculated you and your classmates with the smallpox vaccine. You know this because you google, *What did they dose us with that left a round scar?* Back then, they believed Dryvax was successful if it left a scar. The immunization spurred a body response, creating a minor infection in your skin. They shot us. Infected our skin. Called it, *Successful*. Millennials and Gen Zers do not carry this scar because by 1972, they declared smallpox eradicated and discontinued this vaccine.

When you enlist in the military, you'll learn to army-crawl, pulling your body beneath barbed wire with your elbows, wiggling your hips as you worm your way.

All the while your TI shouts, *Ladies keep your asses low*, and *No one cares if you have a derriere*.

You wonder about the true contagions of war. Still, they pump you full of influenza, meningococcal, varicella, tetanus, diphtheria, rubella, measles, mumps, and pertussis. This is one of your first stops when you arrive at Basic Military Training, some moment between shedding your civilian clothes and pulling on combat boots. All recruits line up. All you do is line up. You march together to meals, to bugle calls, to field drills. Of course, you march towards injections. They never consider that here you are—recruits from all over the nation—a petri dish yourselves, inoculating one another. Still, you look straight ahead as you hand them your arm, your ass, your tongue.

When you reach your first assignment, they issue you a government driver's license and teach you how to top-speed a government vehicle down the center of a runway to check for aircraft braking action.

Slam on the brakes, and, *Document everything*, they say.

They reinject you or hand you pills, tell you, *Stay healthy*.

You nod. You swallow oral polio vaccine, birth control, your tongue. You take another hit of rubella and typhoid, and the most recent influenza. At some point, they test you for TB, usually the PPD skin test, and together, you wait for the immunologic response. Later, much later, when your husband flies missions over Bosnia, he contracts TB. They add TB Monovac to your list of injections.

To keep you safe, they say.

When you enter war, they brief you on local customs. You wonder if you'll shop off-base. Wonder about the type of dining available in the center of conflict. In Turkey. In Iraq. They add another typhoid stab, along with yellow fever. They fill your palm with P-tabs. Pyridostigmine bromide.

Anti-nerve agents, they say.

Pre-treatment for war, they say.

Later, in your 40s, you research that 21-tablet blister pack, that pill you took every eight hours. You discover it protected you from Soman.

In wartime, you no longer care. You take it in your arm or your ass.

You think, *I'm immune to napalm hits of love and war.*

Think, *I was taken down before I entered this world.*

You want only to crawl back through your mamma's exit womb, into soft waters that held you before you were afraid, before you needed vaccinations.

Here, you near 60. Here, you are a mother. A grandmother. Here, decades of dosing and you know your body is built from antibodies. You line up. Here, 2020 and you sit in your personal vehicle at six am. The pop-up vaccination station is a series of tents. Verification. Documentation. Waivers. Here, you remember all those waivers. All those years. You wonder who signed you off in elementary school. You hang your arm out the window, your left because you're in the driver's seat. They shake their masked heads.

Pull down your mask, they say.

They jam the longest cotton swab on earth up your nasal cavity. Your eyes water.

Don't sneeze, they warn.

All you want to do is sneeze. You wait for your quick test to indicate, *Negative.* You rehang your left. They inject Moderna. They hand you a tiny card with the batch number. You think of all the batch numbers on your military International Certificate of Vaccination, stamped by the US Department of Health and Human Services, est. 1798.

Later, your eyes flare.

Episcleritis, they tell you, and, *Most likely stress.*

You fall in line. No. That was the old days. You fall into memory. The time you returned from war, 1991, and your body grew blisters around your irises.

The flight surgeon said, *It's just stress,* and, *Try to rest.*

Your thigh bones hurt so bad you believed someone jammed a blade into each. Then and now—lumps and growths and inflamed tissue and non-diagnosable medical challenges. No one in your genetic line suffers your ailments. Yet comrades in your military lineage could be your sisters. You wonder if the world is our testing ground, humans turned guinea pigs. Preventative care given through orders and obligation. You wonder if the risks outweigh benefits. You wonder about the benefits. You realize there is no thin blue mat. No soft landing. You realize that you've been trained. No. Your body has been trained. Trained to soak immunoglobulins. Trained to look straight forward. Or away. Still, and, somehow, you keep your grip.

Hand-Off

Kristy and I sleek. That's what we call it—our relay hand-off for the 800m medley. Our baton-exchange—her hand to mine—seamless. You might say that you can't tell where I begin and where she ends. It doesn't hurt that we—Kristy and me—are besties. Doesn't hurt that we spend our summers tanning on rooftops, kissing boys, and practicing that hand-off—sprinting telephone pole to telephone pole down the dusty streets of Wheatfield, Indiana.

Here, 1980, we're freshmen entering the high school portal. Still, we race. We race through halls, handing off a pencil or a note. Sometimes we just tap our palms like a secret handshake.

Teachers stop us, *Slow down*, and, *Ladies! Walk!*

Peers move aside, dramatically pressing their bodies to the lockers.

We stay over at each other's homes. No. I stay at hers. We sleep in the basement. No. We don't sleep. We bake brownies at three am. Mid-bake, we pull the pan and add walnuts. Mid-bake, we pull it again, sprinkle chocolate chips or dollop spoonfuls of peanut butter. We build thick-layered lasagna—ricotta, mozzarella, Parmesan.

We're great at everything, one of us says.

We scarf till morning cartoons, usually *Tom and Jerry*. We scarf the way teen girls snuff desire and hunger and hurt.

You should know, there's a secret to flawless baton transfers. The runner receiving the baton bolts, full on, eyes three feet ahead. This same baton-receiving runner cannot look back, cannot slow down, cannot worry if the runner behind her will do her job. That job—one singular focus—is to catch the runner in front of her.

In high school, I cut my own hair. I did this throughout my military service. I still do this today between touch-ups. At some point, Kristy decides, *Cut mine*. I do. At first, I clip half an inch, create soft layers to frame her face.

She looks in the mirror, says, *Nope*.

You hate it?

No. It looks rad, and, *Cut more*.

I trim another inch.
She holds the hand mirror. Shakes her head.
More? I ask.
She grins. She nods.
Make me punk, she says.

We—Kristy and me—don't listen to punk rock, but we believe we're edgy. We wear miniskirts with leg warmers and high-tops. We braid a small strand of our hair and leave the rest hanging loose. We listen to Tom Petty. We sing out loud on the school bus. In Wheatfield, we're wild. So we think.

I leave an inch all the way around. Spike her hair with green Prell gel till it stands.

At school the next day, our classmates ask me, *Why did you do that to her?* and, *I thought you two were best friends?*

Her mom is mad.

Her dad barely notices.

I love her more.

I love her guts.

If you're the runner receiving the baton, you shoot your right arm back, fingers glued together, thumb wide. You create a cradle between your thumb and first finger. The baton is slapped into that web. When the baton hits, you grasp and go, though you are already going.

One overnight at Kristy's, we sing "High Hopes." When I say, *We sing,* I mean we bounce on her bed as I wail, *Hi-i-i-i-i-i-g-h,* over and over. We hold our bellies and fetal into breathless laughter. We sing this song because Laverne and Shirley sing this song. They sing this song with arms looped. We call ourselves Laverne and Shirley, though we aren't sure which one of us is which one of them. When our laughter settles, I re-wail. I want to keep us happy. I want Kristy to laugh always.

The 800m medley involves four runners. Kristy runs the second leg, a 200. I run the third leg, a 400. Kristy hands off to me. I'm the receiver. I remember we broke our school record. I remember us—Kristy and me—crediting our time because of our flawless hand-off. Our record still stands today, over 40 years later.

After I join the military, I visit Kristy while on leave. We drive to Indy for a U2 concert. We pause to buy cherry brandy. We pause to race with shopping carts.

When I tell you, *Race*, I mean that I sit in the basket of the cart and Kristy pushes me, dodging cars as we weave through the parking lot.

We laugh.

We cry.

We miss each other.

We miss each other even when we're together.

In relaying, the baton pass can prove fatal if done incorrectly, costing the team seconds, medals, disqualifications. The mistake most make is in the delivery. One hand misses another. Or the runners can't match one another's speed. This lag forces a loss. Inevitably, someone drops the baton. We—Kristy and me—probably transferred that baton over 100 times in competition and 1000 more in practice, not including our hallway and street sprints.

We never missed.

We never slowed down.

We never dropped that baton.

Not once.

Piggybacking the Smallest Wrestler

Between cross-country and track—winter season—I train with wrestlers. To you, I might look driven. To me, I want that firm, round ass. I also want to avoid home. With the wrestling team, I blend. I piggyback the smallest dude up and down bleachers with the best of them. I V-up. I wheelbarrow. I wear baggy sweats while running gym laps. No one hits on me. No one dares. My brother, David, two years ahead, would knock the shit out of any guy who looks at me wrong.

After the bodywork, we—the wrestlers and me—hit the weights. The machines are old-school and Weider-like. Leg extension. Flat bench. Lat pulldowns. My legs are muscled but shaped like chicken legs, so I work harder on my calves.

You have 400 gams, some guy once told me during track.

I don't think, *Genetic predisposition.* Don't think, *I'm designed to run, not body-build.* I believe you reproportion mass, beef up your backside or lower legs. I believe, *Train and you 'become.'* Maybe I still believe this today, treating my prose like sets of hack squats. If this is true, I've mastered fitness, beauty queen heels, and watercolor. I've also mastered disability, trauma, and brushing the undercoat of Newfoundlands. I guess if you live long enough, you have time to excel at most things you love and all things you're given.

Coach P. is the wrestling coach. He also coaches cross-country and teaches health and nutrition. He's not the coach—the boys track coach—who showed up at my home at ten pm when I was alone.

No.

Coach P. is the coach who asks the class, *What'd you eat for breakfast?*

Most answer, *Pop Tarts,* or, *Fruit Loops,* and Coach follows up with, *Whole milk or skim?*

When he points to me, I say, *Toast.*

Butter?

No.

No?

Nope.

Coach asks, *Jelly?*
No.
You ate dry toast?
Yes.
What kind of bread, wheat or white?
Wheat.
You ate dry wheat toast for breakfast?
The class laughs.
I couldn't tell them, *I ate dry toast because I cook for myself.* Or, *I ate dry toast because that's all we had.*

Here, I speak truth and wonder why Coach doesn't believe me. I've learned earlier, *Best not tell the other truths.* Like the truth about the boys track coach. The truth about what Daddy does to me. The truth about what my adopted brother did as well. No way I can own up about skipping lunch to buy track spikes and cheerleading Keds. Still, not telling feels like lying.

By 14, I bench my weight—116—for a set of three. This is 1980, before girls with muscles were fashionable. Instead, we cheer, spreading our hands in jazz positions, rooting for the boys. Yes, I am all of this, too. And still, I'm the only female sweating alongside the wrestlers. The only chick pushing plates and curling dumbbells. After school, the other girls adjust their hair ribbons and roll sticky strawberry lip gloss across their lips. Love's Baby Soft lingers long after they board their buses.

One afternoon, Coach pulls me in front of the team.
Boys, how many V-ups do you think Becki can do?
20. 30, they say.
How many do you think you can do? he asks me.
150. Clean, I say.
Let's go, boys. If she out-V-ups you, you owe me three miles.

And I do. Of course I do. By 50, they drop. I keep going, another 100, give or take, out-V-upping those near-men as if my life depends on it. Maybe it did. Maybe it does.

Later, at 18, I'm in boot camp, San Antonio. Our female flight is attached to a brother flight—troops of men instead of women. My TI pulls me out of formation, marches me to our brother flight's dorm, tells their TI, *My girl can out-push-up any of your boys.* I wear drab green fatigues belted two notches too tight. My TI counts cadence, holding us low to the ground for an extra beat.

By 30, half the brother flight falls out. My biceps cramp. I press into the balls of my feet, using my combat boots for extra grip. By 60, only two brothers remain. My lower back spasms. My arms numb. I'm certain that I'll smash face first into the asphalt. By 70, I'm the only one still at it.

My TI taps me, says, *Well done, girl.*

Between high school and today, I understand the way I belong in the world. The way I fold into these crevices with men and boys. Understand that most women do not like me. Understand that I'm an outlier—not quite veteran enough, disabled enough, Jewish enough. When I say, *Understand*, I mean that I accept. I accept the way women leave me uneasy—no matter their kindness—I have trouble aligning. No. I have trouble trusting.

Today, I'm the mom of boys. Three. All grown. All larger than me. All kinder than me. I've wrestled and weight-trained and toilet-trained them. I've piggybacked them up and down stairs, in and out of life, through pretend Nerf gun wars and real-life violence. I've also taught them to say *Thank you*, and, *I love you.* They know how to crank the garbage disposal, bake a loaf of challah, and the importance of deadheading—not plucking—flowers.

Sometimes, I say, *This is enough.*

Re-Womb

If I rebirthed, I'd return as an orca and dance with my pod—us three—female, calf, escort. Perhaps I'd be the female, stifle humankind in the Strait of Gibraltar, remind man of his place, his fragile femur and filament, and remind him—every. single. man.—*I am royalty.*

Or perhaps I re-womb, tunnel myself within and without. The darkness but a blanket—a blanket fort, a blanket of snow, an electric blanket. Me, cocooned and healing. Here, I snip stitches and strip screws. Here, I tenderly pull thread and metal. Here, my surgical reparation of heart and bone. I allow my body to finish her job. *Oh!* How she knows. Knows more than I.

I hope when I die, I leave an imprint, not just an impression. Not the pressured outline left on my bed. No. A signature of my stories, my songs, embossed beneath the skin of those who damaged me most. My words flaming through that cage, the place they held me

    hostage.

Snow melts.

    A blanket returns

        to fiber.

            One flicker extinguishes darkness. Think, *Small candle that someone, somewhere, lights in*

    memory of

or in hope for

    or in celebration of

another

> *and another*
>
> *and another.*

    Maybe I do not return as a female orca. Even while they sleep, they guard. Vertical "resting" buoyed by water.
    I wonder, *Does a mother ever rest?*
    Perhaps I un-womb, return as words—a language still unspoken. One that you feel before you note the shape of it leaving your lips. Before your tongue presses to the back of your teeth. Like song. Like whale humming. Like vibration massaging your weary bones.
    Think, *Cello against your chest.*
    Think, *Babe turning in your womb-waters.*
    Think, *Hummingbird in your heart.*
    You no longer feel the boundary—where you end and all else begins. *Oh!* How we have forgotten. We are instruments and whales and wings. I, as language, will swoop through hearts like storm and ocean.
    Think, *Dervish.*
    Think, *Cliff diving.*
    Think…

anything that sets you free,

> brings you warmth,

reminds you

> that you, too, are all of these.

What if Your C-Section Inspired Your Child's Need to Escape

Raise your hands if you have young children who climb out windows, the Rabbi says to us, a small group of single Jewish mothers.

I laugh out loud until half—perhaps 15—raise hands.

Now, keep your hands up if you've had a C-section.

The Rabbi barely glances from his book.

Two hands lower.

The Rabbi moves from behind the small podium, weaves between us, hands flailing as he continues:

Your thoughts, every thought, while your child formed in utero transferred from you to them. The way they exited your womb and entered the world was also an influence. Everything—thought, experience, energy—shaped their little personalities, built their traits.

I'm here, Saint Paul, Minnesota, November 2011. My sons, ages three, eight, and ten, remain back home in Idaho with my friend, Esther. I'm here because Esther secured a scholarship for me. I'm here because she knew before I knew that I needed a break, needed support, needed one night to sleep four hours all in a row.

As you read this, you might wonder, *Nature versus nurture.* I'm certain this debate launched with Cain and Abel. Began with Eve asking (most likely herself), *How could one of my sons hold so much generosity while the other carries a capacity to kill?*

Did she bother asking, *How do we all hold so much?*

A better question, *What pushes us to hate, to allow jealousy to brim over to the point we act out?*

And what about the transference of ancestral wounds? My grandmothers'? My grandmothers' grandmothers?

I raise my hand, ask, *Can I undo my pregnancy thoughts? The bad ones that I pushed into my sons?*

Religion is little if not the opportunity to infuse guilt.

My first-born, Zach, arrived broken in body—deformed hands and feet, visually impaired, defective heart, deaf. I once listed in my journal all of his medical anomalies and, next to the list,

I penned a second list, this one of my contributions. Every bit of his suffering was surely my fault.

Great, I think. *Now, I can blame my pregnancy thoughts, too.* Truth?

I freaked throughout my first pregnancy.

I wish I would had learned to rest.

I still wish I could learn to rest.

Every pregnancy—all three—I over-exercised. Over-nested. Over-cleaned. I painted, then re-painted. I bought baskets and containers and label guns and reorganized. Everything. I color-coded clothing, lipstick, my spice rack.

My first pregnancy was the most intense. It ripped through my psyche with wind speeds up to 300 mph—violent, shredding cars, turning broken debris into lethal weapons.

Throughout those months, I thought, *I'm not qualified. And, I've never changed a diaper. Never fed a baby, babysat. Never rocked or sang or swayed. My baby will certainly perish in my arms. Me, unknowing mommy-me.*

Throughout that pregnancy, I read every book on babies. I attended classes and courses and workshops. Reread. Re-attended. I think, to date, I've completed the *Parenting the Love and Logic Way* course at least seven times.

You can't, the Rabbi says.

He searches my face, controlled but wavering on crumbling.

He continues, *After learning this, you now understand their challenges. You now know better how to guide them.*

I stifle a laugh.

If he only knew the way my sons have guided me.

I once confessed, *My sons have transformed me on a cellular level.*

This.

Truth.

How much courage they poured into me as they stretched and distorted my belly. How much energy as I rose at one and three and four for feedings. How much hope I soaked in our post-op all-nighters—changing bandages, squeezing ointment into stitched eyes and wounds. I felt my ancestors' feet stagger in sand, babes on backs, as I hoisted one infant on my left hip, the other—with the extra weight of casted feet—on my right.

Today, in our kitchen, my youngest, now 16, rolls beef into meatballs and drops them into a crockpot. We take turns adding my grandmother's secret ingredients—garlic salt, ketchup, and grape jelly. We vow to tell no one the recipe.

"Thunderstruck" comes on Alexa, I air guitar and burst the lyrics and my son pauses, I swear, a meatball mid-air.

When did you learn those words? he asks.

When I was younger than you. I keep strumming, legs wide, flopping my head so my hair shimmies like a rock star.

After, we take turns shouting songs for Alexa to play: Squeeze, The Cure, Led Zeppelin. Here, the strange and magical fuse. I know I played music on the radio as we rushed through errands. I understand a mother's influence on culture and tradition. Yet not one of my sons enjoys gardening or prayer or painting. Still, these are my daily meditations. All three boys have snuck bacon double cheeseburgers, though here, I'm a kosher-keeping Jew in the center of Star, Idaho.

We know so little of inheritance.

We know so little.

This morning in prayer, I ask that my boys absorbed only my good thoughts while in my womb, shifting out of embryos and into men. I ask that I poured enough love through each umbilical cord while my body hosted them. Even more love once they entered the world.

I wipe my face, wonder, *Why am I sweating?*

Realize, *I'm crying.*

Notice that I'm swimming in gratitude for each son, for all sons, all daughters. Notice that I forget the way I remain umbilically connected

                                                  to all.

Sticks for Gears

You flew into town the night before I handed Zach over for surgery—his first of 40. He weighed four pounds. He was barely three weeks old. This, 2001. This, one of your three visits. You sat silently with me in that waiting room, the tips of my fingers raw as I shredded fibers off the armrest.

Here, 2025, his latest surgery, and I still tug soft threads while waiting.

Here, a different couch.

A different surgeon.

Zach's 24, 175, a man.

I realize we—you and I—haven't visited in seven years. I think of you and the way we imitated Bruce Lee chops. The way you caught my fists in your palms. The way I caught your laughter. Our tucks and tumbles turned us into something sturdy, something steady. Our childhood yard held more sand and gravel than grass.

Remember?

You shared your Matchbox cars with me. You helped me align and realign those hot rods, over and over, parking them along the edge of your bedroom wall.

Remember?

The way you pushed me on our rusty swings, so high the chains quivered and I swore I kicked through clouds.

Remember?

The way you pushed me, told me, *Speak up.*

Told me, *You're the good one.*

Here I wonder

if you've steered clear because you feel
     you've failed
          me or you
               or the addict whom you mentor
through your church.

I wait.

I won't think of Zach under the knife.

Won't think of all that could go wrong.

I twirl the threads. *Cotton? Nylon?* I notice the wear on these armrests. *How many came before me? How many more to come, to wait on a loved one's heart repair?* Now I remember I wanted to tell you that my damage is not your fault.

Tell you, *It is not my fault either.*
Tell you, *Even our mother couldn't keep me safe
      from her husband.*
I wanted to say, *I miss driving that palm-size Black Beauty.* Lee's '66 Chrysler LaBaron.
Say, *I miss humming like the Green Hornet.*
I miss buzzing 'round our worn Cedar Lake carpet. Miss building pretend cars in our makeshift backyard sandbox, pumping twigs like gears and turning tossed-away cottage cheese lids—our steering wheels.
I fray fibers.
I wait for Zach.
I wait with this dethreaded armrest
      and I miss you.
I miss letting you win.

Earthworms Fatter Than the Year Before

I garden.

I garden until I fill.

I garden until I fill three lawn bags, loving that we use a single trash can. We—our family of three—three sons (and me), three pups (and their mamma), and one calico (who counts as three). Our bin, half full, holds plenty of room for three more bags poking with raspberry branches, five-foot cosmos, seven-foot evening primroses—all those beings I mean to restrain. Here, they tangle through groundcover and grapevine, and look, purple concords the size of my thumb pad.

If I tell you, *I measure by the flat space between my middle two knuckles,* I mean that this space equals exactly one inch. I discovered this inch during Basic Military Training. At that time, 1985, we measured everything. They—the military—required items be flush, grounded, folded into inches. Our tees, six-inch squares. Our hangers, evenly spaced. I found it easier to measure from a section of my body than to pull a ruler. Some females never changed their clothes, which meant never re-measuring items on display and ready for inspection.

I garden, and I find a gold cucumber and several Thai peppers beneath overgrown volunteer horseradish. I don't recognize her as a cuke at first. I research her. My sons and me, probably the pups too, all sit circle 'round our table.

Someone asks, *What is it?*

And someone else, *Can we eat it?*

This, our common question.

The remaining veggies—cukes and bells—shrivel beneath the overgrown horseradish, and by summer's end, they return to ash and dust. The earthworms fatter than the year before. The ladybugs confused. Still, they, the ladybugs, find their way into the house and onto my new quartz countertops.

It takes three minutes to walk from my back kitchen door to my garden beds. Another three to clip what I need for dinner—basil or sage or cilantro. Three to return. Three to rinse my clippings. My little jaunts. I usually forget an item or three—chives or sorrel or Mexican tarragon. All this, part of my fitness regime. You might think this too work-infused for an enjoyable meal prep.

I think this a reminder,
This is where we all begin.
This is where my body will end.

I garden and my sacrum clunks. I can't tell you if it thunks as I bend or squat or stand too long. I can't tell you if my back gives way in the morn or eve. Can't tell you much except I spend the next three days—give or take—with that *zap* and *zing* singing from hip to knee.

We're told that the best remedy for back pain is movement—backbend or downward dog or cobra. But who arches with a squawking back?

I yoga 20 minutes most days. A routine I curated based on my spinal limits and chronic pain. I call this routine, *Water Flow*. I play Sinead O'Connor's "Thank You for Hearing Me" on repeat and leave the tune whispering till my youngest shuts it down mid-afternoon.

On days I can't move, I don't yoga.

These seem the hardest.

On days I can—move, that is—I pull my body into soft shapes, hold, breathe, and say, *Thank you*, to the gods, to this body, to those earthworms toiling through soil on my behalf.

I garden and find my heart buried beneath my fallen lavender bush, a new one sprouting next to her.

A bush, not my heart.

I won't know this at the time, but I'm broken over last year's dead rosemary. This broken arrives now in heaves and tears over the late lavender.

I tell myself, *Calm down.*

Tell myself, *There's a sprout already.*

Tell myself, *It's not your fault.*

I've no clue I'm still mourning the loss of my rosemary and all she's offered—oil rubs 'cross flat strips of zucchini. Her sensual essence 'cross my tender wrists.

By spring, a sprig of her—my rosemary—sprouts one box over.

And now I cry for her resurrection.

I also cry as I dig out those stillborn lavender roots. They stretch for continents. I cry because I know, *This is my fault.* Too ill last year to tend to my garden, I failed to offer a cutting, a clipping. I lay her limbs in my fire pit. Set her alongside cherry and peach branches.

83

Someone asks, *Can we eat lavender, too?*
I think of how we consume.
Everything.
I tell myself, *Waft her*—my burning lavender—her calm and healing into the world. Chant a prayer or blessing or spell. Let her drift towards the haters, the hurters, the healers.
Wait.
Let me change this spell.
I circle her vapors with my hands. Press palms to lashes. Soak her mist into me. Plant a garden in my bones. I build a flower bed off rape and lust and lies. Regrow a lavender bush, one that blossoms gentleness out of my womb, stretches and re-births through spindles and spine, healing me and
    perhaps my three.

Thanks for Sharing the Armrest

I squeeze between two of my three sons in the balcony's first row. My middle son sits with the rest of the college graduates below on the stadium floor. Beneath his gown, a Tommy Bahama button-up, a tie, belted slacks. He's nothing if not crisp, clean. To my right, my youngest, 6'2", 15, and fidgety. His legs splayed and still, his knees press into the plexiglass panel in front of us. To my left, my oldest snaps pictures of his brother, texting them to everyone he knows, *My little-big brother is so smart.*

I wear crimson, wide-legged trousers. I wear these because they don't roll when I move. When I say, *Roll,* I mean my pant leg twisting 'round my own. I wear these because they also hide my lower right leg brace. My soft, patent leather shoes, also red, curve into the shape of my feet, bunions and all. My heart thumps somewhere near my temples, a mix of pride and hunger because I skipped breakfast in our rush.

On the way here, my oldest slept in back, mouth wide, softly snoring. My youngest rode gunshot. He called it. Here, his knees rub the dash. They—his knees—push against everything as he, my son, adjusts to his own rapid growth. Supple, like my shoes, my car's dash has made way for my boy's comfort, the vinyl frayed, the underbelly foam scattered in yellowed bits on my mats.

After the ceremony and once home, I toss aside my brace. I exchange slacks for leggings, blouse for my softest sweatshirt, so thin it's nearly transparent. Here, my own adjustments begin. The seam on my right legging rotates inward, and as I walk, I yank my pants back to center, rearrange the crotch, pull the waist high so my britches bunch into my crack, which I hope will help them stay in place.

It does not. Help, that is.

Over the last three years, I've asked friends, *How often do you adjust your leg seams?* Most smile sweetly, change the topic, order a to-go box. But I have that occasional friend who looks me square and says, *All the time.*

When did you notice this? I ask.

Just now. Because you asked.

You've probably picked your outfit based on this, I say.

For example, I say and point to her bell bottoms, *Those easily align. But if you wore jeans tonight, especially skinny jeans, they'd wrap 'round your thighs as you move.*

She nods. She sips ginger beer. I tear chunks of baked pretzel and dip into honey-turmeric mustard.

The discomfort turns violent, I say.

Like how? she asks.

I'm telling you, I stop, mid-step, sometimes in the supermarket's entrance or center lane or parking lot. Cars brake. Traffic trails 'round me. I kick my right leg, as if to shake off a small, hyper-humping dog. I'm sure I groan or say, 'For fuck's sake'. I'm even more sure that others honk, even those without cars.

At some point during my son's graduation, I notice my shoulders.

Not bunched, I think.

My arms relax on each armrest, my wrists limp, my traps low. My body unstrained. No. Comfortable. Unusual. For me. I want to lean into each son, one and then the other.

I want to whisper, *Thanks for sharing this space.*

I don't.

The auditorium quiets between the moment a name is called and the hoots of family and friends that follow. I sit taller, believing something in my parenting went right. These young men will not be one of those armrest hoggers on a flight. Perhaps this is why, mid-ceremony, my eyes well.

I should tell you, when they were toddlers, my sons took mud baths in the spring. After clearing our garden bed, I added fresh dirt, turned on the hose, let the water flow.

Hop in, I would say and, *Rub some mud in your hair, your pits, but not in your mouth.*

Two would dig in—my oldest and youngest—squealing and eventually turning the activity into a wrestling match. My middle son—the graduate—allowed only his palms to hold a splotch of earth. I have a picture of the boys mid-mud-event, my middle son's belly exposed and spotless, a look of horror 'cross his face as he watches his brothers.

Throughout his toddler years, my middle boy needed his socks adjusted. When I say, *Adjusted,* I don't mean pull them up. I mean the toe seam.

The lines, Mommy, he'd say, kicking off his shoes.

I'd rush over, center the seam 'cross the top of his toes and move to the next need.

Last year, I swear, mid-step, I suddenly understood my seam-moving problem is a gait issue.

Initially, I thought, *This, probably because of my fallen arches or my crumbling cervical spine.*

Maybe my extraordinary bunions, I modify my thinking.

My big and little toes turn inward. I don't blame them. My feet have endured a life of squishing and pressure. Pointe shoes, track spikes, combat boots, six-inch heels. I can't tell you if, in my youth, I ever purchased my actual shoe size. I can tell you that today, I'm a perfect eight-and-a-half. Wide. I can tell you that after slowly sipping brew or chai or juice, I gently roll my toes, mid-phalange, outward.

I tell myself, *This should help.*

Before we leave the graduation ceremony, my oldest reminds us, *We need pictures.*

We pose in a row in front of Gate C. The rain drizzles softly, as if rinsing away an invisible layer of discomfort. My trousers loosely sway as I wiggle my way between sons. All three bigger than the year before. All three larger than me. We ask a stranger to take our photo.

Wait, my tidy graduate son says. He tilts his cap. He smooths his tassel. Twice. We lean into one another, into each other. I grin so hard my cheeks cramp. My eyes water. My heart fills. I reach down, tug my trousers, then allow my seams to fall where they will.

Cooking Instructions

We serve family dinners on Sunday afternoons. My mother invites our pastor, his wife, the youth director, along with any churchgoers she manages to gather. They—the guests—are here bearing witness to our family, built on adoptions and fosters and always, always staged.

This is mid 1970s and Daddy is a deacon. My mother, a recovered Jew. (Her term.) I would tell you our religion resembles confusion, chaos. We build these Sunday suppers from cans. Our meal-making process means opening and draining and mixing. One Sunday, we centered the menu around canned ham.

As we prep, my mother says, *You know, if you eat this, your blood will turn black.*

Rings of pineapple—also canned—cover the ham, a maraschino cherry (from a jar) placed within each center. We mix that popular green bean casserole—condensed cream of mushroom soup, Durkee fried onions, and French-cut green beans. All canned. The fruit salad—not a salad—contains colorful mini marshmallows, Cool Whip, and one can of heavy-syruped fruit cocktail. Even the croissants burst from cans. *Thank you, Pillsbury.* We consumed enough processed food that, to this day, I'm certain I'll need little embalming.

I teach myself to cook from the instructions on the back of boxes—Kraft Mac & Cheese and Rice-A-Roni. I pair these entrees with bags of Nacho Doritos and a two-liter of generic soda. I'm 10 or 12 or 8. By 16, I live alone and save for weeks to invest in *The International Book of Cooking*. I want to become a great chef. I want to become great. I assemble recipes, adjusting ingredients based on my limited pay ($2 per hour) from Burrell Color Labs. I work the night shift after school, after sports. I teach myself to modify: Leave out fancy items like cashews, berries, chocolate chips. Replace oil or eggs with applesauce.

I discover the true value of butter. If you want flaky croissants or crusts, cut in cold butter. Real butter. I save another few weeks for that good stuff. Here, 1982, I live in a studio apartment. No stove. No oven. Only a fifth burner and microwave. By the time I enlist in the military a couple years later, I can curate a five- or six-course spread using an electric teapot and crockpot. I boil or poach eggs straight in the kettle. I fit a metal strainer into the kettle's opening and steam pasta and broccoli. I bake biscuits and cakes in my crockpot and invent one-dish casseroles.

By 19, I rent a home with two other Air Force friends in the small English village of Long Crendon. I spend my off-duty time working my way through that cookbook. I test the recipes. Every. Single. One. Even the non-kosher meals. Especially these. Maybe I hope to turn my blood, turn it black. Or simply untether myself. Prove, *I am not my mother.*

I am not her, my mother.

I left violence. Left home at 14. Left again, a violent marriage, at 42, this time with my three sons and a duffel stocked with medical supplies. Not true. I also snagged my laptop, my computer tower, and a file box of tax documents. I guess I feared the IRS as much as my then-husband.

Four years after fleeing that marriage, my neck collapses. Unable to work, I, no, we—my sons and me—become houseless. Also not true. My sons and I qualify for Section 8. Thanks to military training and my teenage years of budgeting, I navigate menus like I would flight plans, resourcing food stamps, food banks, and hope. I pull in my earlier deployment skills, those times I curated meals out of MREs, turning cardboard crackers into something softer, something I could digest.

After I fled, he—my now-ex—kept everything: the house, the cars, the money. He also kept my personal belongings: my lingerie, jewelry, and dishes. He sent along a few items—cracked outdoor pottery and piles of unpaired socks. The court finally ordered him to return the few items I wanted. The boxes sat unopened for months before I finally garnered energy to rummage through. The first box I opened held my precious manuscripts, scattered, one on top of another on top of another. I delicately set pages aside and below the piles, I found my cookbook. I might've squealed. Did I tell you this cookbook is the size of a small tabletop?

She, returned to me.

I return.

From scratch, I roll tortillas, challah, ravioli. I stretch my welfare dollar. I begin again. I attend free gardening classes. I save seeds from cukes and peppers. I plant onions and potatoes once they sprout.

And we grow. My sons. Me.

We still grow.

Oh, but I can't forget those Sunday-after-church staged meals, plotted with all the right words and all the wrong goings-on. I swallowed back bile the entire time, knowing later, after dark, Daddy will enter my room or bath. I kept scissors beneath my pillow or behind the extra rolls of toilet paper. I never did use them. Perhaps I never understood that I could. Protect myself.

Today, 2025, before I prep a fête, I wander through my backyard garden. I snip basil, sage, and chives. I pluck a handful of raspberries and strawberries. Hummingbirds and dragonflies flutter 'round. I note another volunteer—someone the birds dropped in—a Black-eyed Susan beneath the lilac bush.

If I'm transparent, I'll tell you, *I carry shears outdoors and sleep with a can, yes, a can, of mace in my nightstand drawer.*

Tell you, *I shower only in the middle of the day, the sun grounded, centering sky.*

Tell you, *I'm guarded by Newfoundlands and angels – and Oh! My sons are too. And I am clearly, clearly nothing.*

Nothing like my mother.

Forging

At seven, I trace my mother's loopy handwriting. I don't know this then, but within a couple years, I'll learn to forge her signature, allowing me to leave the school grounds with my fourth-grade teacher for lunch. This lunch, my award for winning the spelling bee. And this lunch marks my first bite of a BLT club. Layers of thick tomatoes, real mayo, and yes, salty bacon. I don't remember worrying about my mother's warning, *Your blood will turn black if you eat pork*. I do remember wiping grease from my chin with my bare forearm. And I remember my small bites, my wish that this lunch would never end.

As a kid, I practice reproducing my mother's frilly letters, working her gaudy G the most. High point. Fat and fancy spiral. This is the '70s and elementary school curriculum still includes handwriting. Here, teachers correct in red, re-working our letter shapes. I think of my mistakes as badges of honor because I hold my own style. No. My mother's style, but I don't know this yet.

I trace her writing, laying a lined sheet over her name. I squint to the pattern of her letters. I realign the lines. Wait. This isn't right. Not her name. I imitate my Great Aunt Gladys' name, though technically, she is not my great aunt. She grew up in the same orphanage as my grandmother, my mother's mother. I pull Gladys' name off the bottom of a check, though I don't know that this is a check. Don't know the way we pay bills, pay each other in this long-handed fashion. Don't know how to address an envelope or raise the flag on our mailbox. I do know my mother's hand.

Why write Gladys' name?

I work through this question, find a child's justification, *Grown-ups probably copy each other's names the way I copy my mother's.*

Later, high school in the '80s, I print square and small, much like my friend Chrissy. Over the years, my handwriting shifts, shapes into life story. My first love, middle school, my letters spin into thick ovals, twice the size of others. I restructure words, like LOVE into hearts or WAVE into, well, waves. By the time I enter the military, I quit signing *Becki* and pen *Rebecca*, reinventing myself. The R at my name's beginning turns large and lingering.

I guess this is why they call it, *Signature*.

Call it, *Your mark*.

One afternoon, early high school, probably a Saturday, I cut grass beneath a window of our small house. When I say, *Cut*, I mean with scissors because we don't own a lawnmower.

From inside, my mother cries, *Please don't leave me*.

You're a fucking thief, Daddy says, and, *How will you feed your kids?*

He emphasizes, *Your*. He says this softly. I know this soft voice. I know what's coming. A stone fills my belly. I swallow back bile and keep clipping. It took another ten years and a war to recognize this heavy pit lodged somewhere in my throat as pity for my mother, not love.

Later, much later—like in my 30s—I learn that my mother was fired from her insurance job. For stealing. For forging checks. Here, I remember Gladys, I wonder, *How much did she take from Gladys too?*

By 2010, they—the American education system—quit cursive from Common Core curriculum. This means my sons can't read my journals. This means the next generation loses some brain development and synchronicity. This also means archives of historical notebooks will eventually be lost like many languages—Gallic, Slovenian, and Plains Apache.

I write longhand in journals most mornings. My penmanship's a mix of block letters and cursive. My penwomanship, finally my own. I transcribe and transfer phrases, flash and micro ideas, out of journals and into my computer filing system. Sometimes I choreograph this work into something more, something larger: an essay, a memoir, a poem, a line. Over the years, I've curated my writing habit, created a practice. I slow-write, much like my slow reading. *Lectio Divina*. In my common journal, I copy other poets, soak their lines. I hope their language will absorb into me. Turn me into a blend of someone else, someone better.

This morning, 2025, I journal and notice my big G. The start of a sentence. I'm surprised. Not by the G itself, but that it is no longer my mother's. It isn't Chrissy's teeny, boxy G either. I remember in grade school longing for a G in my name. At the beginning, of course. I wished I were a Gina or Gabrielle or Gia. *Oh!* To pen a capital, cursive G. Every. Single. Day.

I wonder how many sentences begin with a G. In this essay? None. A big G is a treasure, a rare opportunity and here, on this singular morning, I realize the way I've adopted my own. Soft ink. Round letter. Paper built from tree and ash. I pause. Sit with the weight of my pen. I love moments like this. Moments where the sun starts her day, my journal, open. My heart open as well. Moments I recall, like swiping bacon grease from my chin with a teacher who believed in me.

My thoughts call too soon.
My hand moves.
I sort through my heart.
I tangle with all that I am.
All that I am not.

I've spent most of my life intentionally unbecoming my mother—left home at 14, left an abuser at 42, protected my children from violence, avoided pork consumption, and yes, stopped stealing (another story for another time). Here, 2025, I'm near-60 and just releasing my mother's hold on me. Releasing this hold one letter at a time. Now my own curves whirl and coil 'cross my pages; they knot and twirl, like a hummingbird in flight.

Sometimes I'll stop, ask, *Whose writing is this?*
Sometimes I'll understand that it is not the handwriting.
It's the writing.
And then I'll ask, *Who's writing this?*

Afterwards

Your husband, the good one, the one before the bad one—
your husband and you lean over the edge of rooftop parking. Both
of you panting, him holding his side. Bags from holiday shopping
strewn near your feet. It's December, 1997. From this balcony,
you watch four men meet in the center of the street below as if
each of them advanced from designated corners of a boxing ring.
Moments before, you stood in that center. While in that center,
one of the men, the one with a red beanie pulled over his ears, had
moved towards you, hands waving, *Hey man! I need directions...*

Your nape hairs had risen. Two, maybe three seconds passed
before you bolted. By five seconds you pushed to full speed,
shouting over your shoulder to your husband,

Run!

*

The thick mucus plug splats at her feet as she opens the door,
hands on hips, mouth open, the nurse's call button still blaring.
2002 and your son, ten months and not even ten pounds, splays
over your thighs face down. One gasp of thick air and then

a silence that reminds you of that three-second pause—the
quiet that follows a bombing. The shush before your ears begin
to ring. In that three-second lull, you wonder if you've lost your
hearing. Or your mind. Perhaps your own gasping breath moves
into rhythm with something ancient like the undertone of your
ancestors, until

a wail

from your infant son.

The nurse asks, *How did you know to pound his back?*

You can't remember lifting him, placing him, flattening the
heel of your hand between his blades, dislodging the plug that
blocked his life force.

You shrug.*

Turkey, 1991. Land and sea ebbing and flowing with starving population. You ride in cargo aircraft loaded with crates of supplies and take your P-tabs as directed. Travel includes Batman, Sinop, and Silopi. Yes, there's a station called Batman, like the superhero. At the entrance of one tent stands a yellow sign with black letters, *Gotham City Hall*. And beneath that, *Police Dept.* and the Bat symbol painted in black. Military humor.

In your dreams, you'll remember this boy, his belly bloated, his gaunt face haunting you. His eyes manage to sink and bulge at the same time. You hand him an orange and it floats above his palms, his arms splayed on outstretched legs. His skin taut across jutting bones and you want to help him *open* his treasure, peel the rind. You tap his shoulder. The orange rolls. It rolls first. Then the boy. Topples. Boneless. One tiny heap. You kneel beside him. Lay him flat.

Shout, *Help*.

Tilt his head. Place your ear near his mouth. Look at his chest. Look for the rise.

Search for the fall.

You retilt, pressing his pointy chin to sky. His skin thin, fragile. His eyes glazed, unblinking.

You ask, *Where's his mother?*

You ask, *Where's someone who knows what to do?*

...one

and

two

and

three

and four...

You press his chest, one hand over top the other. Knuckles calloused, fingernails bitten. Sweat drips between your breasts, slips over your nose, into your eyes till the boy blurs, into cloud, into white sun. And he was beautiful and peaceful and still. Beautiful.

You did not pause.

Maybe he'll return.

You're not crying.

It's only sweat.

Did someone say, "*Let him go?*"

Did someone say, "*You tried.*"

*

Mid-bite, mid-forkful of salad—well, iceberg with a crouton, if you call that salad—you feel the heat. Everyone's watching you. Your brother. His two toddler sons. His wife—though she is not looking at you—holds her face and sobs. Next to her, her 90-something-year-old grandmother who reaches across the table and pinches a chunk of chicken off the red-checked cloth. The piece that only a few minutes ago blocked her airway.

You don't remember the trigger. Surely something in your peripheral.

Your brother asks, *What just happened?*

You keep chewing—lettuce, garlic crouton, honey mustard dressing—stabbing your salad, stabbing your mind.

Here, 2000, before you birthed children, but after you failed the boy. Here, you remember rising, walking over, lifting Grandmother from her seat. You remember thinking, *Gawd, don't break her.* Then, one thrust (or was it three?) with your fist and that chicken chunk thwacks, hitting the table. You remember settling her gently into her chair, returning to yours, adding some pepper because the salad sucks and now, now your nephews clap their hands.

*

Summer, 2022. You press your lips over nose and mouth and suck first. The pup still wet, still sticky, still. *Is this the seventh? The ninth?* You lost count after six pups and now, the rest of your family sleeps. The pup, so still. Too still. When nothing comes from your sucking, you blow quarter-puffs and watch its tiny chest lift and lower. Barely a pound, the pup fits in your palm. Its paws push towards sky and you think, *Final movement,* as something inside turns heavy. The Earth pauses her spin. The air is at rest. Somewhere in another room, the fridge hums, the house creaks as she settles.

You hear yourself, *One and two and three and…*

on *four,* the pup's paws pedal into a squirm and you scurry for scissors and snip his umbilical cord, swipe your face with your forearm, wiping sweat, slime, tears.

You whisper, *Five.*

Somewhere in Star, Idaho, Between Rage and Comfort

Rage flames in unspoken dialogue, like the time I almost said, *I'm not afraid of you,* to my now-ex, his fist near my face. Flamed when I stood at attention, knees nearly buckling, alone with that commander, both of us knowing why he called me in.

Rage lights a torch for those who suffer needlessly. Remember those refugees? Remember the way we coaxed them down that mountain? We promised to keep them safe. Then we left. We left them. Remember the boy, the boy, the boy?

Rage blazes as my son uses his debit card at the local gas station for a simple purchase—vitamin water and M&Ms. Blazes as the person behind us releases another loud sigh, says, *Why can't he just get this?* Blazes while they speak in hushed tones, but my hearing-impaired adult son hears them, his hands shaking as he punches in his PIN, one of his many independence goals.

Rage flares while doom-scrolling videos of missile launches, burned babies, raped grandmothers, and the 19-year-old hostage with her foot chopped away. And those flares erupt, something near my heart, near my temple, as I continue scrolling (I can't quit) into comments, and read, *Serves her right,* and *Finally,* and *You asked for it.*

*

Comfort swells like warm vanilla and English-style caramels. Swells with smooth, silky turmeric teas infused with honey, ginger, and a splash of pepper, steeped in my hand-shaped ceramic mug, a heart etched into its clay.

Comfort dances with backyard ladybugs and dragonflies. Dances with sticky soil thick with earthworms and my gifts of eggshells, coffee grounds, and bits of banana peel.

Comfort means my airway keeps clear of foreign objects, of bits of salad going down the wrong pipe, of small toys, and bile. Means my worry over our next meal or gunman or prescription price shelves itself. Means when I wake, I'm unperturbed by spilled coffee, muddy footprints, my leg paralysis.

Comfort presents in my kitchen, in the next page, in the pause to pet a pup. Presents in the dervishing candle flame. Presents in that single line I revise and revise and revise and, in surprise, I find the word. That one word. The only word.

When all else fails, I control my pen, orchestrate words. No. I follow phrases as they trickle from heart to page and often, in storm's center, I remain unruffled.

*

Driving center lane, my heated seat on high, a truck pulls close, and the driver raises his fist, his face crunched, his mouth, mostly teeth, shapes into a square. I can't make out what he says, but I can guess. I look 'round, think, *Maybe he's angry with someone else.*

But there's no one else.

I'm not sure what I've done, but I'm certain I'm to blame. Here, my cheeks burn. Here, my forehead beads. Here, I wonder, *What if…he jams into me, pulls a gun, accuses me of…*I can't think of an accusation, but I'm a single mom and the sole provider and somehow, I must survive this drive.

Later in my car and steering much slower because my rear right tire has flattened and now flops. I've missed my teaching gig with the juvenile detention center. I head to Les Schwab for repair. I up the heat on my seat.

At the intersection, a truck pulls close. Not the earlier, square-mouthed-fist-pumping-driver truck. A different one. This truck pauses, the passenger-man rolls down his window and waves. He wears a full beard, a flannel, and a smile as he yells, *You have a flat*, and I grin, though a bit too broadly. I'm warmed. I'm warmed to be warned by some strange man. My face flushes. I swell with gratitude. I live in this small town where neighbors pause, still keep you safe and some strangers wish to help and now I wonder if the previous fist-pumper offered a gesture of victory, thought me a comrade, or maybe his dog just died.

I drive.

I drive slowly.

I pace my heart to the *thwack, thwack, thwack* of my flat tire.

I lower the heat on my seat.

...Sauntering...

High school, I read and reread paragraphs. Not because I loved what I read, but because I didn't understand. I jotted words in a thin, spiral-bound notebook, found them in my Webster's— emancipation, degradation, adulation, confabulation—said each aloud. I tried to teach myself smart. After a while, I tired from pausing every other sentence, so I skimmed. I wish I could tell you that I listened to my teachers. Wish I could say that I watched historical films or documentaries back then. Wish I could tell myself that I paid attention to the way words sounded.

I did not.

I thought myself a daydreamer, my mind distancing itself from any task in front of me. Classroom lectures turned into background noise. I nodded. I transcribed. Later, I would page through my notes, squint, sort through my line-by-line nonsense.

Washington was a real ladies' man. Over six feet tall.
What does height have to do with love? Wait.
Wooden teeth? Women find this attractive? My stepdad has false teeth. So does my mom. They keep them—their teeth—in glasses of milky water on the bathroom's...
Wait...Washington...

Some nights—still today—I read only a paragraph before bed. I might reread the same lines four or five more nights, as if I could spoon phrasing into my mind to remember. After the birth of my oldest, now 24, I quit reading at night. Books blurred.

Oneintoanotherintoanotherintoanother.

I understand now what I couldn't grasp then: Stress jumbles the brain. I spent my son's first year with subspecialists and surgeons. By the age of one, he'd already endured 13 surgeries and spent hours each week in therapies: physical, occupational, developmental, visual, and speech. I spent those hours with him, feeling far more disabled than he.

Before I became a mother, I became an airman. I checked out books from the base library at RAF Upper Heyford, England, stacked them to my chin and wove my way back to my dorm. I prided myself on my 100-books-a-year challenge, considered myself an avid reader. By winter, to reach my book count,

I selected the thinnest, easiest reads off the shelf. Over time, I found the only way I could retain information was to rewrite entire texts. I copied—word-for-word—every line, slowly and methodically, as if my hand could absorb the knowledge my mind hungered for.

When I stumbled upon unfamiliar words, I highlighted them, and at the end of a chapter, I returned, recording them in the back of my journals, creating my own glossary. By now, you'd think I have garnered some massive vocabulary—eight years of military study, five years in undergrad school, six more years to complete two graduate degrees. I note-took my way through academia and life.

It did not help.

I am not smarter.

I'm not sure when I noticed, maybe mid-20s, but my struggle shifts from misinterpretation into mispronunciation. My linguistic ability feels spattered and sputtered. Even the simplest word stirs trouble. Common names. Places. Well-known brands. Maybe other self-taught, avid readers face this same dilemma. Or maybe it's just me.

My grandmother once told me, *Your mother left you in your crib all day* and, *You were almost two before you walked* (another story for another day).

I tell you this to emphasize my early stunted development. To showcase that perhaps this lack of interaction in my formative years might've delayed my vocabulary maturation.

Perhaps my choice in reading versus listening—the page instead of audio—limited my connection to phonetics.

Perhaps two years in speech therapy in third and fourth grade strained my genioglossus. Here, I wrestle to press my tongue high, struggle to stretch each side because they tell me, *Touch the inside of your upper molars* to produce an R sound

Perhaps now, shaping words feels like chewing leather.

Perhaps my brother dropping me on my head when I was a toddler, knocking out one of my front teeth, shaped my lisp and fear of exposure. When I say, *Exposure*, I mean the gap in my grin, which birthed self-consciousness. I rarely smiled, which most likely contributed to some odd atrophy of my eleven lip muscles.

Four years ago, I dated Paul Michael Glaser.
While driving, he says, *Put a cork in it*.
When he says this, he means my mouth.
He says, *Bite a cork with your teeth and speak clearly*.
Says, *Move your lips and tongue around the device*.
Says, *Americans are lazy talkers*, and adds, *You're one of them*.

I take this advice seriously and within two minutes of articulation training, my jaw cramps.

I don't stop.

I still do this "training."

I've other skills that have surely helped shun and shape my annunciation inability, like my love of foreign films, which means subtitles. Or my time in service, stationed in England, surrounded by blokes who re-sounded words such as aluminum, schedule, and vitamin into a new dialect.

At some point, I believe I have dysgraphia, dyslexia, or aphasia. I watch rap artists, my mouth dangling, perhaps drooling, while I witness the speed at which they spew phrases. I long for some level of that automaticity. Long for my brain to disengage while my mouth and mind decode with less effort.

But one Sunday, I lounge in a chair, turn the final page of *All the Light We Cannot See*, my journal opened to where I'd rewritten my favorite lines. I spread my ink-stained fingers and stretch—my palms, my neck, my jaw. I love the way I retraced Doerr's poetic map, his dance with language. I can't tell you how many Sundays it took me to finish "reading" Doerr's work. I can tell you that my entire body turned to glitter. I can tell you that I overflowed with that satisfaction of finishing something even when it takes months or years. I slowly smile, maybe even automatically, at last embracing my language-meditation, my slow walk across the page. Finally, I hold this moment close, knowing this too, a gift.

Feather Sweeping in Gary, Indiana, 1986

You think, *Grandma*, and you might think raspberry jellied cookies, chicken soup stocked with more flat egg noodles than meat, a soft hug that reminds you of a butterfly.

I think, *Grandma*, and I'm reminded of borscht so thick you eat it with a fork. Reminded of the sticky bile at the back of my throat as she ground slimy slabs of meat and whole onions into the most delicious chopped liver. Reminded of her Folgers can sitting on her stovetop, half filled with schmaltz, the main ingredient for most of her recipes.

You think, *Grandma*, maybe you see her silhouetted in a rocking chair, darning socks or mending hems or painting a thin line with dark nail polish on her hoseless legs. Drawing that line from her heel to the tender spot at the back of her knee. You want to remind her, *This is 1976*. But you're too stunned and fascinated to interrupt her ways.

I think, *Grandma*, and I remember my first visit after enlisting in the Air Force. Remember her handing me a disposable Daisy razor. Remember her saying, *Shave that peacoat*, as she pointed to my Air Force overcoat and I thought, *She's lost it*, and, *Not surprising after all she's endured.*

- Her mother left her—not quite a year old—along with her three siblings on the doorstep of a Jewish orphanage.
- Sally—the oldest sibling—took on guardianship, finished raising her younger siblings once she aged out of that orphanage.
- When she—my grandma—became a mother, she gathered her children, loaded them onto the train to visit her mother, their grandmother.
- My uncle, one of Grandma's children, once told me about these visits. Told me how the howls through the halls of that institution still haunted him.
- At some point, some thugs took a hit out on George, Grandma's husband. I heard it involved debt. Heard it involved gambling. I think there was a war as well, which is safe to say, because isn't there always a war?
- I should mention, *She's Jewish.*

You think, *Grandma,* and you probably recall pink lipstick over-outlining lips, rouge too dark and too circled and too high, and hair ratted into perfect beehives.

I think, *Grandma,* and I see her in unexpected places, like that moment on the train. The woman in front of me with her fake-furred collar and her coat buttoned to her chin, her eyes crinkling as she smiled. Those eyes told one story, while the trace of Loreal #5 Red revealed another. I saw her as *Grandma.*

I know her as myself.

I think, *Grandma,* and I think of her frustration after I declutter her pantries. When I tell you, *Declutter,* I mean tossing cans of beans with expiration dates almost three years old. I mean family-sized shampoos and conditioners lined in rows, dust so thick I wipe them to read the labels.

I ask, *You know you live alone, right?*

She laughs and shrugs and says, *I don't want to run out.*

Later, long after she passes, I find myself in Section 8 Housing with my three sons, my youngest just over a year. I foodbank shop each week. I snag extra shampoo and soap and, after a year, my shelves resemble Grandma's.

I think, *Are we ever that different? One from another?*

I think, *Grandma,* and I remember the way she sent me home-baked chocolate chip cookies packed with popcorn, *To keep them soft.* How she included tiny hand-beaded pins and bracelets in all those care packages. She shipped those boxes to England. To Spain. To Turkey. She followed my whereabouts and later, I told her, *I devoured all the cookies,* and, *I ate the popcorn, too,* and, *Nothing ever tasted so good.*

I think, *Grandma,* as I long for our brief encounters, like holding hands as we flashlight search, brushing corners with a feather through her tiny home in Gary, Indiana. We sweep till we find every last breadcrumb, and later, much later, I learn from my uncle the way she mapped and plotted and hid those crumbs herself.

Grandma

Grandma

Grandma

Play Me Some Willie

Curtis pulls brined chicken, only dark meat—legs, wings, thighs—because *They hold more flavor,* he told me earlier. He places the parts in a disposable foil pan, one we've repurposed for the last three weeks, give or take. He douses the meat with half a cup of hot sauce.

Most people use eggs, he says, and adds, *But my grandma taught me that this is a better binder.*

He doesn't say, *We have no eggs.* If he did—say this—he'd mean, no eggs here, Deployment, 1991.

He'd also mean, no eggs then, the years with his grandmother.

We stand side-by-side, Willie Nelson wailing from Curtis' boom box. Someone sets up the card table. As friends—new and old—arrive, they stack their goods: opened bags of Lays, half-full bottles of Hennessy, packs of cigarettes, jars of mayo and pickles and mustard. Someone brings preboiled potatoes for the potato salad. Someone else delivers refrigerator biscuits that we "bake" in a cast iron pan on a fifth burner.

We each bring what we have.

Some gatherings, we offer little.

We offer only ourselves.

What is this twang? Someone pauses Willie. Someone else exchanges one cassette for another. If it were up to me, I'd listen to Kenny G and Sinéad O'Connor. Curtis prefers Skid Row and Nelson.

Curtis mixes flour and cornstarch, salt and pepper, and, when we have it, garlic and onion powder. He places the chicken, piece by piece, in a used but clean gallon Ziplock, adds a cup of the flour mix, seals and shakes.

He dips his fingertips in vodka or water, drizzles it over the large stockpot quarter-filled with oil—usually canola.

He tells me, *Peanut oil creates the perfect crunch.*

Before Curtis finishes cooking, we pass shots of Tequila 'round. We teach one another our latest moves on our makeshift dance floor built from duct-taped cardboard boxes. Our bodies sheen with sweat and desire as we circle one 'round another, 'round another. We find our places and plop onto the concrete floor, used paper plates in laps. The first bite of that chicken is the best—buttery and flakey.

Pie like, I say, and I can't stop myself, can't stop licking my fingers.

I'm out of uniform and in baggy overalls, one shoulder strap undone, my white tank a nice contrast to my war-time tan.

And I'm the only one.

The only white girl in our friend-group.

Still, I feel my belonging, here, with my brothers, my sisters. With Curtis.

Tomorrow, I'll weave through the war to my flight planning job, perhaps I'll even plot their route home, carried away in the belly of some C5.

Them.

My war-time friends.

My war-time lover.

And still, the war will carry on,

long after I leave,

leave those refugees to starve out

and remember Curtis, his soft lips and softer heart, the way he pressed me into him when we danced.

And, yes, his perfect fried chicken.

*

This morning, 2025, I tell Alexa, *Play me some Willie,* while I squeeze grated potatoes through a cheesecloth.

Make sure there's no juice, I tell my son. *That's the secret to binding latkes.*

Did anyone ever make potato juice, you know, as a drink?

I think they call it vodka.

And we laugh. My youngest, 16 and 6'2", hair to the center of his back, removes his earbud, says, *Alexa, play "Fortunate Son."*

I love this song, I say.

My boy stands over our meat counter, finely grating onions. He places a wet dishrag next to our butcher block, his way to prevent tearing up while chopping onions. We add panko, eggs, kosher salt, and pepper to our potato-onion hash.

We cook over a gas flame in my cast iron skillet, one of many artifacts that followed me from war and into several states until finally settling here, Star, Idaho, 26 years ago. We have a blend of oil—basil and peanut—that sizzles when my son flicks water from his fingertips.

Grandma taught me that trick, I say, and immediately realize, *No. Curtis did.*

I don't correct myself.

I wonder if it matters—who passed along which recipe, which skills, which secrets.

I tug the waist of my jeans which cut into my thickening middle. My hands, now veiny. My skin so thin it's nearly translucent. The aroma of my grandson—a blend of baby powder and sweet potatoes—still lingering in my wiry, greying hair from his morning visit.

I love that leftovers gift more than repurposing a meal. I love that my grandson and my grandmother have both brought something to this dish.

>*Can you ever hold someone too long?*
>*Can you hold someone too long?*
>*Can you ever?*
>*What?* my son asks.

I laugh, unaware I spoke aloud.

As friends arrive, I navigate our kitchen, route through courses. I carefully plate slices of grilled chicken, fennel salad, pickled herring, applesauce, and these perfectly crisp latkes. I nod.

As I arrange food, I'm reminded of the way the human heart needs to hold itself through tradition, whether in the center of conflict or crushed into a heavy red state. No matter…we hold onto only a few things.

We need to eat them all, my son interrupts my thoughts.

We both know that he means, surrender.

Means, enjoy.

Means, there is no trick to "keeping them warm in the oven" or "fresh on a wire rack."

We understand that delicately fried food is best served immediately. We gather—my sons, friends, and me—and someone asks, *Where's the ketchup?*

Don't you dare, my son says midbite.

Unlinear Me

2014 and I color outside the lines, a pencil or crayon or thick marker rubberbanded to my right hand, securing the device to wrist and fingers. My then five-year-old sits beside me, his tongue pressed to one corner of his mouth in concentration.

Everything within me hurts.

No.

I carry pain only in my unnumbed spaces.

I am unable to feel either hand from shoulder to fingertips, though, on occasion, electric shock blazes through. My teeth chatter. My body sheens with perspiration—upper lip, shins, lower back. After a few seconds, my brain registers, *Pain*.

My body's always done this for me, this pre-notification.

I'm holding (not holding) plum or gold (my two favorite colors) in my right hand. I love these hues pushing against each other. Love their oppositeness. They sit 'cross the color wheel, 'cross the skyline, 'cross a dragonfly's back. In this juxtaposition, beauty lives

like hurt and love

fire and ice

puppies and gaslighters.

Never mind.

There is zero beauty regarding a gaslighter, no matter what or who you push them up against.

Along with my unfeeling arms/hands/shoulders, my lower right leg hangs lifeless, emotionless.

You can do it, my five-year-old says as I try. Try to color.

My tongue darts from one corner of my mouth to the other.

Please stay between the lines. Please stay between the lines, I will my rubberbanded pencil/crayon/marker.

Tears hit, splatting my page, puckering some girl superhero's almost-purple cape. The gold boots and belt weep into

amber – ochre – sunrise – twilight.

Here, on my page, her cape shifts into flight. The edges—where there are edges—wisp away from margins, from lines, from containment.

Here, my superhero's bodiced body shifts into cloud and ocean.

I want to puncture my coloring page. Want to stab through these lined/aligned containers.

I wonder, *Who decided the woman's body should shape into an hourglass?*

Who voted that straight lines on the jaw, the eyebrow, the waist are gendered masculine? Some man (I'm certain) somewhere invented our culture's hip-to-waist ratio. The ratio that now crosses math and architectural lines turned into a standard, a goal, a requirement for beauty.

Oh! The ways I've dishonored my athletically-lined, unlinear me—
      stretched and distended my belly with gorges,
          emptied self to bones and filament,
              and still, I felt fat,
feel fat.

But at least I felt/feel
    something.

There is little better than the weight of a good pen resting on the pad of my middle finger. No need to squeeze or grip. We simply glide.

Now, I color. I color without the weight of solid pen. I color with my son.

He reminds me, *You're doing great.*

He lies.

No.

He is not yet jaded with society's limiting beliefs. He is unaware of our social stay-between-the-lines laws.

He, a natural enjamber.

He leaves me
        with wonder,
        with anticipation
for the turn at the end of his line,
        like glitter and rain.

Before my hand-failing moment, 2014, I called myself an artist. My charcoal sketches half-decent,
    my watercolors
roaming 'round the page, rivering into whatever
      they needed
      to be.

That's the gift of watercolor,
    of water.
In art, I know the way to release.
If you try to control a line—or anything—you lose.
    You lose the art,
                  the essence,
                                 the possibility.
I lost my art,
    my essence,
        my possibility
trying to hold lines.
When I think of plum and gold, I see Van Gogh—not one painting—like *Sunflowers* or *Starry, Starry Night,*
    but all. His works mesh and crush into one another for all of time.
His whimsical bend
    and lack of lines.
Look.
    Close.
        Closely.
Are there ever any lines?
One speck juxtaposed against another and another and another
    from a distance
        seems a line.
Aren't we all—everything—simply atoms in continuous motion?
There is no line to color outside of.
        There is no container for breath or heart.
Keep going, my boy says.
And I do, I really do, knowing he and I—two specks next to each other—meet, greeting
    one   another   far beyond
the ocean's edge.

Finding Myself in the Middle of a Row

My first day detasseling, summer between seventh and eighth grade, I wear flip-flops. While walking the field, I trip on a stone the size of a cat, tearing my big toenail from its bed. In the field, you don't look down, towards ground, while pacing through rows of corn. You don't look up, either. You meditate. You pull. Tassel after tassel. You drift through dirt drier than desert as you weave between stalks.

Along with ripping off my toenail, I learn about corn. I learn that there are boy corn and girl corn. I learn that there's four female rows for every male. Four for one. That seems right. The males keep their tassels, preserved and intact, like peacocks fanning feathers. Their boy corn's pollen dust blows into the silks, the satins of the girls. The girls must have their tassels plucked.

This ensures female pollens cannot contaminate sacred cross-pollination.

By my third day of yanking tassels—despite heat—I learn to wear a tee over my bikini top. Learn to cover myself. Those inner rows steam like saunas, ten—maybe fifty—degrees hotter than weather in our regular world. I cover myself, though I want to bake and tan and brown into another nation. I cover myself because those girl-leaves cut like machetes, leaving slashes across my belly and arms. I cover myself out of need for protection from the other girls.

Girls cut like that.

I learn this on my sixth day of jerking tassels. The other detasselers chattering beyond the corn:

I heard she gave it up for Joe.
She only did it with him because he's on the football team.
Not true. She did it with the whole team.
I heard she didn't actually do it but gave the whole team head.
Did she swallow?
Probably. Look how fat she is now.
She might be pregnant.

By the time school starts, the detasselers have spread those rumors, saying that the girl in question had had a baby, or an abortion, or an adoption. Sometimes two. By the time school starts, I'm glad I took that job, there in the field, with the cheerleaders and jocks and heads. Those of us present weren't talked about.

I buy a hat by the third week of detasseling. Tug it lower to conceal my now-bleached-out eyebrows. I keep covered to remain undercover—fly on wall, fly on shit, shit on shit. I wish I had the courage to speak up for the girl. I only learn to stay silent and covered. And later, I'm ashamed of my silence and coverage.

A month after detasseling corn, but still a month before school begins, my scalp—despite my cap—peels from the burn. My hair turns silver-white as though I'd aged, every day in that field a decade. Every day, a lesson in silence.

AfterBurn

In the shower, I unscrew the lid of tar shampoo. I gag. I remember: *Mother.* Her slathering tar-like goop from a small, prescribed tub. Her sores—the size of my palms—scaled and raised. Her body patched across her belly, her thighs, her back.

Until now, I didn't understand the way newly-paved roads forced me to roll up car windows. The way odor eats the best of me. Like that rotten-egg-sulfur smell that thrusts me into darkness, even in white midday sun. My mind floods with images of POW bunkers. We are blindfolded, though at the time, we are only in training. We are somewhere safe and stateside. We are somewhere in the mid-1980s. We know we can feel our way. Feet in dirt. Hands on stone while we inhale fake mustard gas.

We call this, *War preparation.*

Brother, does the war still sting?

Remember that cold shower slap-sting when you were, what... Ten? When you swallowed that entire bottle? After, that bile sting stuck in your throat, thick and mixed with metallic blood taste/smell and you, unsure if that blood came from stomach pumping or acid vomiting.

They poured you out of you.
Emptied you.
As if you could empty more.

Sister, are you still emptying?

The bee sting and wasp sting and brown recluse sting. That one, near your big toe that turned into a bullseye. Those easier stings—sunburn sting, afterburn sting, bleeding ulcer sting because you won't quit hot sauce.

Or worry.
The perineal stitch sting.
And the sting on that stitch when piss hits.
And the mother sting.

Brother, don't you know, she's the worst sting.

Remember?
Your doctor asked, *Who's hurting you…down there?*
And you finally shape words, turn them into something round. You thought the good doctor would gift you a longer hospital stay. Thought he'd pretend-diagnose you with something terminal, something easier. Or perhaps adopt you and, if not, offer you a Dixie Cup of Kool-Aid so you could fade.

Sister, are you fading yet?

Before you reach that final syllable, the long e at the end…
Daddy, Mother stung, *Liar*.
And, *She always needs too much attention.*
And, *She's having sex with boys at school.*

Sister. Brother. The doctor raised his eyebrows.

You lowered your head.
You sealed your lips.
Remember?
You, only nine at the time.
Mother-scent sent soul to nostril to neuron. A single cauterizing memory. Her—Mother—out of the shower, whipping Jergens over her scabs. Later, the next day or next 50 years, you'll whiff that Jergens-scent as a woman reaches past you in produce, selects an avocado, one too long for your taste. Cherry and almond lingers and, once home, you drop your groceries on the counter, step into still-dewy grass, wonder why you need to chop another branch from your cherry tree, wonder why every almond tastes like death, wonder if you'll ever quit flinching
every time you piss.

Tarnished

If you'd asked me in my youth what I thought of my lady parts, I might've responded, *Tarnished*, as if, through use and overuse and over time, I'd become rusted, stained, corroded. I wouldn't have been wrong. The vulva reacts to encounters—bicycle seats, horseback saddles, rapists. Mine was no different. After delivering my first son in 2001, they—my lady parts—darkened 'round themselves. Perhaps pigmenting for protection, blending into themselves.

A way of healing.

Or hiding.

I know this because I mirror-checked my labia before and after my Mona Lisa. If you haven't heard of the Mona Lisa, it's basically a vagina lift. I'd call it a roasting because part of this procedure includes lasering tissue. The labia's extra folds are shrunken much like plastic wrap heat-sealing juicy fruit. Think, *Shrinky Dinks*. The medical industry considers burning away flesh, *Treatment*. Considers inserting a wand into your vagina, *Noninvasive*.

I think if there exists insertion, therein lies an invasion.

Did I mention that you're alert during this procedure?

When I endure fully-awake interventions, such as root canals or Lasik, I pretend I'm overcoming some POW interrogation. You know, push my mind into a happy place. Call myself, *Warrior*.

I could not do this during my Mona Lisa.

Throughout the pinching and searing of my own lips, I kept telling myself, *Avoid re-remembering childhood*. Like the brain game, *Don't Think About Blue*; you only see blue. Instead of smelling my searing tissue, I re-whiffed the stench of Daddy—sour milk and fried chicken. Re-felt his heaviness pressing on top of me. I gripped the edges of the table, pressed my feet deeper into the stirrups, told myself, *I am in a cliinic*. Said to myself, *I am in a medical space*. I might've said out loud, *I am with chrome and machines and soft-pastel painted walls*.

Then it ended.

No sex, the doctor said.

I nodded. *Who would want to copulate after that?*

This includes masturbation. Don't insert anything for a few days.

A few weeks later, I sit with my thighs splayed on my bathroom tile. I grasp my handheld mirror with my feet. It fogs. I think of all those steamy images—dog paws and hearts—the ones I fingered on backseat car windows as a kid. I wipe my mirror and tenderly touch my soft, pink, even-toned me.

You'd think I would have felt elated, even excited. I did not. Instead, I filled with heaviness that I'll later recognize as loss. My badge of honor stripped, as if my earnership of delivering babies out of my body could no longer be proven. My body, this body, built my babies. Their souls chose me, came through me. Now, this evidence that verified me as a fighter and a mother was oxidized. Now, my lady parts lustered, ripe, youthful. A contrast to my five-decade self.

Then I cried.

2001, fourteen years before my Mona Lisa, I push. I don't feel the rip, but I swear I hear it.

After, my OB says, *You tore naturally.*

She says this like it's a good thing.

Later, my friend, Ari, gently sponges my area in the hospital shower, I notice rust rushing down my thighs, swirling into the drain. It takes a minute before I register, *My blood*. I wince while Ari cleans me, while my baby, only hours old, rests on a respirator in the NICU. I wince when I piss. Wince when I sneeze. Wince if I push anything near that tender patch of stitching, bridging one small hole to another.

A year or so before my Mona Lisa, my six-month pregnant friend, Meg, tells me, *Varicose veins are the worst*. She's in shorts and a too-tight tank, her belly button poking like a nipple. I look at her thighs.

Not there, she says.

I shake my head.

My coochie, she says.

I nearly pass out. (I'm sensitive that way.)

Vulvar varicosities, they call it.

Due to an increase in blood volume, they say.

The body's response to pelvic pressure, they add.

My mouth moves, like a prayer, a *Thank you* to my sons.

All three, considerate of me, birthed without this condition.

Who knew how much war and ravaging our lady parts endure.

Here I thought mine special.

Today, evening, Spring 2025, and the world blazes while my heart packs with political fear. Earlier, I dug through Earth's winter blanket—dead petals and leaves—scooping debris as I search for life when a small crocus, her lavender petals edged in cream, pops through. I lean back on my heels with an audible sigh. A vaguely familiar echo pulses through my body. Tears fall. I nod.

I say, *Thank you.*

I say, *Good job.*

I say, *You pushed through despite it all.*

And here, I return to 2015, to cold bathroom tiles, my thighs wide. I imagine my younger self and this version of me pulls her knees together, a small smile spreads 'cross her lips. 'Cross mine. She knows her body is finally hers. I know now, my body, is finally mine. All those men who took me, tore me, corroded my softest places without permission, were also roasted during that Mona Lisa.

Repaired, then and now, I'm certain my vagina whispered, *Go.*
Go now and heal.

Chiseled

It started with a bag of Nacho Cheese Doritos and a 2-liter of generic pop. I don't remember if we called it pop or soda. I do remember I'd just finished Basic Training. This means it's 1985. During my six weeks at Lackland, I live on dry chicken and stiff mashed potatoes, most likely rehydrated flour and paste and not potatoes at all. The purge comes easy. Too easily. I bend over, think about some man. Vomit. No inducing necessary.

I think, *Kinda normal. Kinda natural.*

At some point, I purchase a scale and dropping weight to below 120 becomes my non-military mission. When my weight rises, say to 121, I buy a box of Correctol from the base exchange, gulp three tablets and, within a few hours, I shit water. By morning my cheekbones chisel and eyes hollow, and I note my brow bone, which I'd never noted before. My eye shadow dips, curving into new territory—luscious, sultry.

Like all addictions, one hit pivots into three, then 30, then too many to count. My binges grow into buffets, increasing with two, sometimes three bags of groceries.

Who knew the stomach could distend so far?

Who knew it would ever return?

I'd retch till my abs cramp. Curiously, I maintain a six-pack.

Puke-crunches, I call it.

My new weight mission shifts: 110.

Within a few months, those three pink tablets no longer deplete my face into the dehydrated look I learn to love. I find myself gulping an entire box—24 tablets—that pink-chalk coating offering me a pre-gag. My supervisors witness my gorge. Witness my wasting, too. They think me anxious. Think me dying. They fail to intervene. In the military, you cannot break or crack or shatter. But you can shrink. I remain fake, whole and boned.

One time, after my binge and purge and box of laxatives, my body couldn't quit. Could not stop her emptying. My kidneys did. Quit.

Renal failure, they called it.

I weighed 100 lbs.

I stood before my full-length mirror, rubbing my palms over my jutting hips, twirling slow and model-like. I glanced at my back ribs. I slid on jeans—size zero—without unfastening. Still, my body held inches I can pinch.

I found a new mission: Below 100.

My heart palpitated.

Potassium deficiency, they called it.

Later, much later, I would think about the way starvation offers more than a sense of control or feeling thin. It gifts an eternal longing to die. A slow and tedious path to suicide, one less morsel at a time. Food settling on your tongue or stuck in your bowels seems an invasion. In my moments of small satiation or minor fullness, memories of raids and intrusions—men infiltrating my child-body, my woman-body—damage me even more. So, I grew too thin and fragile for them—all of them—to notice me anymore.

Though I hoped they see what was left of me.

Perhaps this illness is simply an act of disappearance, one's fight for invisibility.

Self-preservation through the art of emaciation, I call it.

And it worked.

It really works.

Except for my heart and kidneys.

Cardamon & Caraway

Here, I indulge in India. I'm 24, sharing a house with two other active-duty Air Force members in the center of Long Crendon, UK. Here, early 90s, and this village carries a gentle pace, sprinkled in thatched cottages with honeysuckle-drenched doorways. Think, *Midsomer Murders*, without the murder. The town holds one market, one petrol station, and, at the bend near the station, an Indian restaurant. The only restaurant. I drive almost an hour from base to home. The unlit road winds. Sheep graze near the edge. Blast "Red, Red Wine" or "What I Like About You" or "Troy" and sing, sometimes shout, lyrics. The drive is often the best time of my day.

Decompression.

De-stress.

My personal debriefing.

I sink into garlic naan, the bread so soft it melts before I can properly chew it. The garlic, roasted and shmeared and sweet. Funny the way a roasting turns something sweet. I order biryani rice, slightly spiced with bits of fried onions and cashews fluffed in. I scoop Dal Makhani by the spoonful and later I learn to make my own—onion-tomato base, generous chunks of butter and dollops of cream. Bingeworthy food. The place offers take-out, not delivery. Some nights, I arrive pretending I'm hosting a party back home. I leave with several paper bags loaded with mint or imli chutney, rice with curries and sautéed eggplant.

I tell myself, *I'll share with my roomies.*

Tell myself, *This is for dinner tonight*

and, *Lunch tomorrow and maybe lunch the day after.*

I know that I lie to myself this way.

I spend my time off-duty tucked in a spire atop St. Michaels. Long Crendon sits less than 15 minutes outside Oxford. And yes, you go in the rain, or you don't go. My black umbrella matches mood and sky. I pack a thermos of hot English tea and a tote of books—Voltaire or Turold or Milton—anything difficult to help me feel smart. My glasses, round and large, take up most of my face.

I stay for the day.
Stay till dusk settles.
Stay till my eyes blur and I no longer see the lines.
While here, sharing a house with two mates, I deploy. Morón, Spain. Then Incirlik. Then in and out of Iraq, delivering food and medical supplies to Kurdish refugees. I trade my MRE—chili with beans—for BBQ meatballs and peanut butter. The peanut butter MRE includes crackers. Someone, at some point, invents the MRE Cracker Challenge. You have two minutes to eat every cracker in the package.
Without water.
The two minutes launch as soon as the first cracker hits your lips. You empty the crackers into a bowl or your helmet.
Ready?
Go.
The crackers are drier than crackers. Drier than dirt. They suck saliva right from your tongue. The crackers fly and fall, land in earth and ash. Still, you must eat them. (Five-second rule.) Swallowing is the hardest part.
We all fail.
I like the meatballs because they taste like butter and garlic and rosemary. Later, years later, as a civilian, I buy a meatball MRE, try to re-experience my war time flavors and am saddened with its tastelessness.
I wonder, *Does everything taste better in war?*
In war, I like the crackers and peanut butter because, once down, I keep them down. More accurately, once down, they cannot come back up.
When I return from the Gulf, back to Long Crendon, I invent a whole wheat bread baked with molasses and caraway seeds. I slice tomatoes and layer them thick enough to measure four inches. I eat my sandwich with a knife and fork. Slow eat. I brew strawberries into jam with my breadmaker, adding a pinch of red pepper flakes for bite. My time alone in our house measures in meals: I over-consume and once our fridge empties, I make meals out of flour and sugar and water. I'm creative that way. Crepes are the easiest—on the way down, and on the way back up.
It's here I try to replicate Turkish chai.
My first sip is purchased from a vendor with dark teeth and

crinkled skin beneath a canvas tent, Incirlik Alley, Turkey. I fan fragrance from cup to face, peppercorns, cloves, cardamon, cinnamon. My shoulders level. My breath evens as if I recognize this scent.

Something ancient.

Something familiar.

I didn't know this then, but these are similar spices used for Havdalah—the "separation" ceremony at the end of Shabbat. It is said that during Shabbat, we are gifted an extra soul, and at the end of Shabbat, we relinquish that soul. These aromas, secured in a b'samim box, offer comfort for this loss. I learn even later that chai translates to "life" in Hebrew.

Once home—Long Crendon—I think of my contradictions.

Life and death.

Honey and rot.

In Turkey, mid-war and post-war, I sipped, allowing the tea to linger, coating bitter bile from my continuous purgings. Despite the heat 'round me, I welcomed the warmth of that drink.

Still, today, I cannot replicate that chai.

I mortar and pestle whole cloves and cardamon. Grind a stick of cinnamon. Push granite against granite, creating a powder so fine it's transparent. It's here, today, I indulge. I'm 58, sharing my Idaho home with sons and Newfoundlands. I'm far, so very far, from England and the Gulf.

It's here I try.

Try to return.

Try to remember.

I scoop creamed honey into warmed milk, add my spice powder. Heat on low. Steep till the milk turns caramel. Sit with my books—rain or not—Salinger and Woolf and O'Connor. Some nights, the sky is so clear, I read the constellations and talk to my future self. I talk with my past self, too.

Tell them both, *There is no repeat or rewind.*

I try.

Try to hold the words of the masters.

Try to hold the brew on my tongue.

Try to let the essence absorb the moment.

Only this moment.

Only this.

The Power of a Pseudonym

We—women—spend our 20s, even our 30s, proving to men (and perhaps ourselves) that we can change the brake pads, climb Denali, and still keep our lipstick within the lines.

We—women—fight tooth and knuckle to out push-up the boys, score the highest in high school automotives, teach our sons to pee standing. Teach our sons to heed the sound of *No*.

Or the unsound of *No*
      when *Yes* remains unspoken.

All the while we re-teach ourselves to hear our own voice, our guts, our Nos and Yeses.

We—women—placate the back-stabbing females who feel the need to one-up, undermine, override us because, what, they think they'll reach the top before us?

      instead of us?   in spite of us?

Us—we—the women, who paved their driveways, planted magnolias, delicately placed their grandmother's bones into plots while curating their history, holding space for their ancestors' recipes and wisdom.

They—the confused youth—have forgotten, there's only more ash and dirt at the summit.

They've forgotten how thin air bursts your lungs when you've reached the peak.

(Still, they believe there's an apex to reach.)

We—women—were young once. We, too, wasted vital years constructing deprivation chambers—living carb-less, sugar-less, love-less—as if a sweet-less life and cinching our belts another notch might give us something better. Give us more. Give us more as we took up less and less and less

    space.

Though our aunties told us, we—women—though they told us, *Don't forgot to allow honey to seep, sit on your tongues, merge in*.

Instead, we swallowed everything fast—opinions, false stats, noxious weeds—until we failed to see the difference between hemlock and mead.

Until we—women—stepped over that line,
> that pile of six-inch heels and smooth skin 'round our worn eyes.

We—women—now glance over our shoulders, noting that the crowd throwing stones is our younger sisters as if we—the aged, the crinkled—turned into threat.

Oh! Our young sisters (who we once were), how they fail to hold our hand beneath sun, a plaid blanket spread beneath the two of us for comfort. These young sisters have grown into mean gatekeepers, worse than the men we measured ourselves against.

They—the youth—will fade into us—the senescents.

And when they do, I hope they'll know the power of invisibility, of a pseudonym, of a solid nap. Hope they'll cherish one noncombative sister who tenderly stands beside them, takes turns carrying their babies through the desert, all the while barefoot, bleeding, and baring bruises.

The Price of Energy

I collect money. Collect it in a mason jar. Collect coins and bills and handwritten IOUs on post-Its. I charge five dollars per bad attitude. I began this transactional system when my sons were younger, say eight and ten and two. The price lower back then. A quarter for an eye-roll, a dime for a, *But Mom.*

A few years ago, I stored this jar, believing that we—my sons and me—had arrived. When I say, *Arrived,* I mean here, someplace stable. Maybe I mean here, Star, Idaho. What I really mean is that I hoped we'd shifted into peace, which meant our energy stabilized.

I believed that arriving here equaled more time. No. More energy.

In my journal, I map my time.

4:30. Feed pups. Make beds.

5:00. Prance through my garden and pluck basil and sage, fry them crisp, fold them into fluffy omelets.

5:30. Yoga.

6:30. Prep lunch—tuna salad pitas with air-fried sweet potatoes smothered in rosemary, again, from the garden.

7:00. Don't forget the laundry, the dishes, the bills. Remember: Prep dinner, shave Parmesan by hand for pasta. Oops. Buy Parmesan. While shopping, buy bread and eggs, just in case.

Already noon.

My sons munch their lunches while playing video games. In another room, I unclog the vacuum for the third time this week and tell myself, *All this energy expenditure will buy me—*

Appreciation?

       Approval?

            Irreplaceability?

Tell myself, *30 minutes. Certainly it will buy me 30 free minutes.*

I brew tea.

Set my writing intention.

I'm lying.

I need an entire week, most likely a month, to polish my manuscript. I need minutes all in a row. And a pup eats the remote, I hand-wash dishes, store leftovers, mop floors for the seventeenth time. I forget my tea as I return to my manuscript. Technology fails. I troubleshoot. I reboot the router.

I hole up in my office for six minutes, rereading the second line of the sixth stanza of a Golden Shovel and
    one of the boys pokes his head in, *What is there to eat?*
    I pretend not to hear him.
    It's six pm.
    Mom? Mom? Mom, I'm hungry, and
        I flare.
        Words escape, *You need to leave*
        me alone.
    The words are louder, more square than I intended.
    The head in the doorway pulls away. Angels gasp. Devils clap. I slump, hold my face. My brain chugs a thousand directions.
    My focus is hard-earned, if earned at all.
    I count, *Oneandtwoandthreeandfour…*
    Boys, come here.
    Look, I say and point to my poem.
    See? I say, and show them my need to maintain the anaphora phrase AND the end word AND
    I'm stuck in the middle of this line on a word that feels wrong in my body, I say.
    How can you feel words in your body?
    I have no answer.
    No.
    I know how to answer.
    I could ask, *Did you feel my shout?*
    But I can't.
    I don't.
    I'm sorry, I say. *I didn't mean to raise my voice.* Though we know this is the nice way of owning yelling.
    Let's make hot cocoa, I say.
    The guilt of parenting quilts me, snuffs out my need to create.
    After they sleep, ten pm, give or take, I wander my home like a ghost. I wish I could re-carve our life, turn time back to last week when we watched a movie, ate salted popcorn mixed with Hot Tamales.
    What I really want is the ability to leave the dishes dirty.
    You piece of shit, I say to me.
    I move room to room and kiss their foreheads, say, *Forgive me.*
    Tell them, *I'll try harder.*

Ask, *Can I have a do-over?*

They slumber.

The next day, I find and place the mason jar on our kitchen counter.

Do you remember our energy exchange? I ask.

You used to charge if we argued with you, one of them says.

Do you remember why? I ask.

Because arguing zapped you and you needed more coffee to parent.

Good memory, I say.

Uhm, but we're not arguing, the other says.

I know, I tell them. *Do you remember how I told you everything requires an exchange of energy? How, in the old days, people traded chickens for flour, or horseshoes for grain. How currency—like money—became a thing and we forgot what it represented. Our energy.*

We have to pay you for something now? one of them asks.

No, I say.

I place a five-dollar bill in the jar, say, *This is for my bad attitude yesterday.*

One of them says, *Maybe you'll save enough to hire a housekeeper and that will help your attitude?*

Genius, I think.

A pup sprints through, dishtowel in her mouth. Another pup chases after. The boys squeal and join in and suddenly, my body,

my body feels the word, and I, too, sprint up the stairs to my office, to my poem, jot the word and plop into my chair as the resistance of stillness fades. I'm here. Me with my body, my body with my words, my body-words with me. I smile a small smile, perhaps a glimmer of achievement.

Decluttering Damages My Writing

I quit decluttering the way some might quit a bad habit. I quit because decluttering became unhealthy for my heart. And my writing.

At first I tried the KonMari method. I moved through my home, tidying by categories, not locations. I offered my stuff a three-pile approach—Dump, Save, Gift.

I asked my stuff, *Do you still spark joy?*

It responded, *Yes.*

I failed at KonMari, so I attempted the "No Contact" method, which meant boxing and separating myself from my goods. I gathered wooden spoons, gift wrap, silk scarves. I stuffed them in boxes. Stacked those boxes in my garage. After three months, I forgot my possessions, repurchasing similar items. Later, I found myself in the center of a new pile, re-sorting duplicates.

My writing—both generative and polished—circulates this same way.

I create mounds of essays and poems, filing most away. My own KonMari or "No Contact" approach. I set aside work only to realize later that I recreated similar poems and essays. I am bogged in a space opposite *Writer's Block*. I call this, *Writer's Overdrive*. My art stagnates in storage. My creative life mirrors my external organization. More accurately, disorganization.

Once I "see" this, I explore the way I move (and do not move) energy.

I understand.

Understand the way I'd forgotten; I'm a memoirist, an essayist, and a poet.

I rely on objects.

My possessions serve as placeholders. I surround my home, myself, my history, through my gatherings.

Here, tucked in a corner beneath my stairway, lives my 6x12 carpet, rolled, leaning.

Marie might ask, *Does this still spark joy?*

I hear myself, *Yes.*

Perhaps she'd step closer, ask, *Then why not use it?*

I find myself explaining this relationship. Explaining the way this rug is more than something to step on.

Tell her, *It is woven with silk and wool and handcrafted.*

Explain, *This is a piece of art.*

Or more truthful, *This is a piece of me.*

I'd add that during the war, while deployed to Turkey, while flying in and out of Iraq to deliver food and medical supplies to Kurdish refugees, I found this rug in Incirlik Alley, a small marketplace outside the front gate of Incirlik Air Force Base.

I'd tell her, *After I bought this rug, I ask an F-111 pilot-friend from my home base if he would "ship" the rug back home, to RAF Upper Heyford, England.*

At this point, Marie's eyes might glaze, but I'd keep talking.

We both know the story is more for me.

My pilot-friend agrees and tucks that rug in his bomb bay, along with pounds of pistachios—the big ones that weren't dyed red or green. Later, like months, still deployed, I build friendships with the Turkish vendors. They teach me the proper way to brew chai and, after, sell me a Turkish copper coffee pot, a double-boiler kettle, and leather outfits that I design. All of these treasures. All transported in those F-111 bomb bays. All of them, boxed and waiting at my home base. Awaiting my return. I still have them. (Not the pistachios.) They've journeyed with me from England to Texas, from Texas to Idaho, in and out of marriages and illnesses and births and deaths.

She—Marie—or you, might call me, *Sentimental.*

Might ask, *If it's so important, why stow it?*

I'd tell you, tell Marie, *It doesn't matter where it lives with me. It just matters that it's still here.*

Decluttering, if you want to call it that, is moving energy. These gems carry energy, and because they hold energy, I consider them living beings. Instead of trashing or donating, instead of asking whether or not this jewel sparks joy, I ask, *Did I allow this being to fulfill her purpose while in my care?*

If the item no longer fulfills her purpose—however defined—I've failed the object.

I've allowed her energy to stagnate.

If you understand stagnation, you understand sewage and mosquitos and disease. If I'm no longer offering my treasure space to be all that she might become, I must release her, gift her to a new caretaker where she breathes freely, where she thrives.

My troves have become life-partners.

That knife on my office shelf reminds me, *Your grandfather cut his way out of a tree, slicing his parachute as he dangled in The Czech Republic after his B-24 was shot down, but before he was taken as a POW during WWII.*

That worn book, though I might never open his pages again, tells me, *Remember? You persevered through grad school. Twice. Despite disability and single motherhood.*

These "things" are more than things. More than "stuff."

They are witnesses.

They invite me back into my life, and, in doing so, they enrich and enhance my writing. Perhaps, without them, I fear I'll forget my history.

Or perhaps, without them, I fear I'll be forgotten.

Maybe our relationship—my treasures and me—means more. Perhaps I know they are *home*, waiting for me each day, and their existence is proof of mine.

Beneath my stairs, my carpet sparks; she offers more than joy. If you look further, under my stairwell, I've a secret room filled with art, bean bags, a small table, and a light. Here, I read or pen longhand. All the while, outside my sacred space, the world keeps her spin, an argument resolves, the tea kettle shouts, pups wag and shatter a coffee mug off a low table. Still here, in my writing cove, I imagine my rug unrolling herself, beckoning me, lifting us away.

Berry-Picking Meditation

I feel him before I see him, fatness and fuzz brushing the underbelly of my foot. I garden shoeless, press my archlessness into soil while I yank weeds, deadhead blooms, snip away unnecessaries.

His stinger punctures my naked sole.

I know a sting. I am unsurprised. Bees swarm my gardens, diving through magnolias, lavender, and cherry blossoms. Tangle in my blonde wisps. I've no fear of bees. They're the least of my worries. I pride myself on the way I attract pollinators instead of predators. (Finally.) The way I unborder boundaries and fence lines.

The way I contribute to flowers.

The way I contribute to the future.

The way I contribute.

I turn my sole towards sky. The bee quivers his last breath into dew. These mornings, my meditations while berry-picking—raspberries, strawberries, blueberries—I need to beat the birds to my fruit. Need to beat the sun to the horizon.

I lift the bee, place him on a leaf-grave and lay him to rest beneath the lavender I know he loved.

Thank you, I say.

I tell him, *Sorry*, for the startle of my sunrise steps.

When I pluck his stinger from my now-tender skin, redness blooms like a dahlia. Somehow, I know to spade mud. Pack earth to my wound and keep moving. Keep blood flowing.

I let poison seep.

Let gravity weigh her work.

After ten minutes, maybe less, the swelling leaves, the sting forgotten. And here I, I wish my body worked this way with mud and gravity. Wished earth would sponge poison-semen and predator-men from within, release my stings, my swellings.

I wish I could dive through lavender on a singular mission, dew watering my wings.

Me, forever in flight.

Epilogue

Listen,
    you believe you've burned away some hurt here, writing these flashes.
    You've done well.
    You faced demons.
    You remembered to hold love.
    Still, you're brand new at this, only beginning to hold yourself.
    Don't—do not—imagine you're through expressing stories, pouring them out of your body and onto the page or yoga mat or garden bed or palette.

    Try to keep going.

        Try.

            Keep going.

    Oh! And try, try to rest.
    Something inside you believes you can. Believes, *You are safe now.*
        [...you are...]

    So go on.
    Sleep hours in a row, head pressing into silk pillowcase, shades pulled tight, a Newfoundland draped over your chest like a weighted blanket
    ...and after, walk barefoot through the morning dew. Gather petals and put them in a basket. Eat raspberries from the bush and hug your peach tree. Twice.
    Tell her, *Thank you.*

        [Tell yourself.]

About the Author

Rebecca Evans is a Pushcart Prize-nominated essayist and poet who writes the difficult, the heart-full, the guidebooks for survivors. Her debut memoir in verse, *Tangled by Blood*, bridges motherhood and betrayal, untangling wounds and restorying what it means to be a mother. She's a memoirist, essayist, and poet, infusing her love of empowerment with craft. She teaches high school teens in the Juvie system through journaling and visual art. Rebecca is also a disabled veteran, weaving disability, military experience, and Jewish heritage throughout her work. She co-hosts Radio Boise's *Writer to Writer* show.

Her poems and essays have appeared in *Brevity, Narratively, The Rumpus, Hypertext Magazine, War, Literature & the Arts, The Limberlost Review*, and more, along with a handful of anthologies.

She's earned two MFAs, one in creative nonfiction, the other in poetry, University of Nevada, Reno at Lake Tahoe. She's co-edited an anthology of poems, *When There Are Nine*, a tribute to the life and achievements of Ruth Bader Ginsburg (Moon Tide Press, 2022). Along with her full-length poetry collection, *Tangled by Blood* (Moon Tide Press, 2023), she's authored a collection-length poem, *Safe Handling*, (Moon Tide Press, 2024).

For Rebecca's essays, poems, and workshops, visit: www.rebeccaevanswriter.com

Acknowledgments

Heart-Full acknowledgement to the editors of the publications where many of the essays in this book have previously appeared:

Brevity: "A Little Letter from an AI Rebutter" and "Decluttering Damages My Writing"

Fiction Southeast: "Writing 'Me'"

Jewish Literary Journal: "Feather Sweeping in Gary, Indiana, 1986"

Lilith Magazine: "What if Your C-Section Inspired Your Child's Need to Escape"

Meat for Tea: "Berry-Picking Meditation" and "Buddy Check"

Narratively: "Finding Myself in the Middle of a Row" and a version of "Writing 'Me'"

The Normal School: "When Fireflies Scatter"

Oddball Magazine: "Chiseled"

My sincerest appreciation to Moon Tide Press and their unending support and belief in my work, allowing me exploration into my narrative expression. To my editor, Betty Rodgers, her keen eye, love, and, above all, patience. To Ken Rodgers, for pushing me with art and co-creating a platform, Writer to Writer, for the love of all artists. To Corporeal, all my heart for the safe and sacred space to unabashedly unleash.

To my sons, my grandson, my daughter-in-law, my heart-found family of love—without you, I would lack the courage to rise, to write, to overcome.

Also Available from Moon Tide Press

Outliving Michael, Steven Reigns (2025)
Prayers With a Side of Cash, Kathleen Florence (2025)
Somewhere, a Playground, Rich Ferguson (2025)
The Tautology of Water, Giovanni Boskovich (2025)
Take Care, Mark Danowsky (2025)
Dilapitatia, Kelly Gray (2025)
Reluctant Prophets, J.D. Isip (2025)
Enormous Blue Umbrella, Donna Hilbert (2025)
Sky Leaning Toward Winter, Terri Niccum (2024)
Living the Sundown: A Caregiving Memoir, G. Murray Thomas (2024)
Figure Study, Kathryn de Lancellotti (2024)
Suffer for This: Love, Sex, Marriage, & Rock 'N' Roll,
    Victor D. Infante (2024)
What Blooms in the Dark, Emily J. Mundy (2024)
Fable, Bryn Wickerd (2024)
Diamond Bars 2, David A. Romero (2024)
Safe Handling, Rebecca Evans (2024)
More Jerkumstances: New & Selected Poems, Barbara Eknoian (2024)
Dissection Day, Ally McGregor (2023)
He's a Color Until He's Not, Christian Hanz Lozada (2023)
The Language of Fractions, Nicelle Davis (2023)
Paradise Anonymous, Oriana Ivy (2023)
Now You Are a Missing Person, Susan Hayden (2023)
Maze Mouth, Brian Sonia-Wallace (2023)
Tangled by Blood, Rebecca Evans (2023)
Another Way of Loving Death, Jeremy Ra (2023)
Kissing the Wound, J.D. Isip (2023)
Feed It to the River, Terhi K. Cherry (2022)
*Beat Not Beat: An Anthology of California Poets Screwing on the
    Beat and Post-Beat Tradition* (2022)
*When There Are Nine: Poems Celebrating the Life and Achievements
    of Ruth Bader Ginsburg* (2022)
The Knife Thrower's Daughter, Terri Niccum (2022)
2 Revere Place, Aruni Wijesinghe (2022)
Here Go the Knives, Kelsey Bryan-Zwick (2022)
Trumpets in the Sky, Jerry Garcia (2022)

Threnody, Donna Hilbert (2022)
A Burning Lake of Paper Suns, Ellen Webre (2021)
Instructions for an Animal Body, Kelly Gray (2021)
Head *V* Heart: New & Selected Poems, Rob Sturma (2021)
Sh!t Men Say to Me: A Poetry Anthology in Response to Toxic Masculinity (2021)
Flower Grand First, Gustavo Hernandez (2021)
Everything is Radiant Between the Hates, Rich Ferguson (2020)
When the Pain Starts: Poetry as Sequential Art, Alan Passman (2020)
This Place Could Be Haunted If I Didn't Believe in Love, Lincoln McElwee (2020)
Impossible Thirst, Kathryn de Lancellotti (2020)
Lullabies for End Times, Jennifer Bradpiece (2020)
Crabgrass World, Robin Axworthy (2020)
Contortionist Tongue, Dania Ayah Alkhouli (2020)
The only thing that makes sense is to grow, Scott Ferry (2020)
Dead Letter Box, Terri Niccum (2019)
Tea and Subtitles: Selected Poems 1999-2019, Michael Miller (2019)
At the Table of the Unknown, Alexandra Umlas (2019)
The Book of Rabbits, Vince Trimboli (2019)
Everything I Write Is a Love Song to the World, David McIntire (2019)
Letters to the Leader, HanaLena Fennel (2019)
Darwin's Garden, Lee Rossi (2019)
Dark Ink: A Poetry Anthology Inspired by Horror (2018)
Drop and Dazzle, Peggy Dobreer (2018)
Junkie Wife, Alexis Rhone Fancher (2018)
The Moon, My Lover, My Mother, & the Dog, Daniel McGinn (2018)
Lullaby of Teeth: An Anthology of Southern California Poetry (2017)
Angels in Seven, Michael Miller (2016)
A Likely Story, Robbi Nester (2014)
Embers on the Stairs, Ruth Bavetta (2014)
The Green of Sunset, John Brantingham (2013)
The Savagery of Bone, Timothy Matthew Perez (2013)
The Silence of Doorways, Sharon Venezio (2013)
Cosmos: An Anthology of Southern California Poetry (2012)
Straws and Shadows, Irena Praitis (2012)
In the Lake of Your Bones, Peggy Dobreer (2012)
I Was Building Up to Something, Susan Davis (2011)
Hopeless Cases, Michael Kramer (2011)

One World, Gail Newman (2011)
What We Ache For, Eric Morago (2010)
Now and Then, Lee Mallory (2009)
Pop Art: An Anthology of Southern California Poetry (2009)
In the Heaven of Never Before, Carine Topal (2008)
A Wild Region, Kate Buckley (2008)
Carving in Bone: An Anthology of Orange County Poetry (2007)
Kindness from a Dark God, Ben Trigg (2007)
A Thin Strand of Lights, Ricki Mandeville (2006)
Sleepyhead Assassins, Mindy Nettifee (2006)
Tide Pools: An Anthology of Orange County Poetry (2006)
Lost American Nights: Lyrics & Poems, Michael Ubaldini (2006)

Patrons

Moon Tide Press would like to thank the following people for their support in helping publish the finest poetry from the Southern California region. To sign up as a patron, visit www.moontidepress.com or send an email to publisher@moontidepress.com.

Anonymous
Robin Axworthy
Conner Brenner
Nicole Connolly
Bill Cushing
Susan Davis
Kristen Baum DeBeasi
Peggy Dobreer
Kate Gale
Dennis Gowans
Alexis Rhone Fancher
HanaLena Fennel
Half Off Books & Brad T. Cox
Donna Hilbert
Jim & Vicky Hoggatt
Michael Kramer
Ron Koertge & Bianca Richards
Gary Jacobelly
Ray & Christi Lacoste

Jeffery Lewis
Zachary & Tammy Locklin
Lincoln McElwee
David McIntire
José Enrique Medina
Michael Miller &
Rachanee Srisavasdi
Michelle & Robert Miller
Ronny & Richard Morago
Terri Niccum
Andrew November
Jeremy Ra
Luke & Mia Salazar
Jennifer Smith
Roger Sponder
Andrew Turner
Rex Wilder
Mariano Zaro
Wes Bryan Zwick

www.ingramcontent.com/pod-product-compliance
Lightning Source LLC
Chambersburg PA
CBHW030221170426
43194CB00007BA/823